PARALLEL BARS

AN INSTRUCTOR'S COMPLETE DEVELOPMENTAL PROGRAM

FOR

STUDENTS OF ALL AGES

by

GARRY L. SMITH

EDITOR
Frank Alexander

TEXT ARTISTS
Dawn Bates and Holger Jensen

COVER ARTIST
Dawn Bates

Published by FRONT ROW EXPERIENCE, 540 Discovery Bay Blvd., Byron, CA 94514-9454

500 BOOKS IN PRINT AS OF 1990

ISBN
0-915256-30-4

Published

by

FRONT ROW EXPERIENCE
540 Discovery Bay Blvd.
Byron, CA 94514-9454

ACKNOWLEDGMENTS

I am indebted to a fellow Instructional Specialist In Elementary Physical Education in the Baltimore County Public School System, Mr. Edwin H. Lanehart, for previewing my first draft material.

I am indebted to Mr. Holger B. Jensen for the outstanding job he did on the original art work on the Parallel Bars Charts.

I am indebted to Mrs. Dawn Bates for the outstanding job she did on the drawings within this book.

I am indebted to Jean and Nick Palmere for their continual support and assistance with many of the "behind scene" tasks.

I am indebted to the Supervisory Staff within the Office of Physical Education in the Baltimore County Public School System for their support, guidance, and confidence throughout my career in Elementary Physical Education.

Most importantly, I am indebted to the thousands of boys and girls who have touched my life thus far within my teaching career. Through their enthusiasm, interest, and sincere sense of caring, I have come to realize that my life's profession was the best choice I could have ever made.

ABOUT THE AUTHOR

Garry L. Smith is an Instructional Specialist in Elementary Physical Education in the Baltimore County Public School System, Baltimore County, Maryland. He holds a B.S. in Health, Physical Education, and Recreation from Lock Haven State University, Lock Haven, Pennsylvania (1972) and a M.ED. (Administration) from Western Maryland College, Westminster, Maryland (1978).

Mr. Smith has organized and taught gymnastics programs in conjunction with the Baltimore County Department of Recreation, Y.M.C.A., Y.W.C.A., and Baltimore County Public School System. He has presented numerous gymnastics demonstrations/workshops at the elementary and middle school/junior high school levels in county school systems throughout Maryland; as well as at various conventions, conferences, and meetings in the northeast, southeast, and west sections of the country. He has received professional awards at the county, state, and eastern district levels.

Garry L. Smith brings eighteen years of experience and expertise in Physical Education together with the talents of professional designers, illustrators, and printers to produce the most unique, attractive, and instructional book for the parallel bars.

CONTENTS

Chapter-10

MOTIVATIONAL IDEAS -- 149

PREFACE

This book has been written to help elementary, middle, and junior high school physical education instructors and other professionals in varying capacities who work closely with young people in parallel bars instruction. I feel it is one, if not the most, comprehensive basic parallel bars books available. The book is an outgrowth of the parallel bars charts produced by PETA, Inc.

It is my hope that the readers will become more knowledgeable in the area of parallel bars instruction, and they will be able to approach the area with greater skill, confidence, and efficiency. While it is true that not all physical education instructors and other related professionals can become experts in the teaching of parallel bars skills, they should make a sincere and professional effort to include the parallel bars in their instructional gymnastics program.

There are ten Chapters within this book. Chapter One includes seventy-four General Teaching Suggestions. The General Teaching Suggestions are the direct result of personal experiences and they are offered as general suggestions to _seriously_ consider when organizing a parallel bars unit of instruction.

Chapter Two contains fifty-four General Safety Rules. Again, the General Safety Rules are the direct result of personal experiences and they are offered as general rules to _seriously_ consider when organizing a parallel bars unit of instruction.

Chapter Three covers Primary and Intermediate Warm-Up Activities And Exercises. The Primary Warm-Up Activities are geared toward students in grades K-2, whereas, the Intermediate Warm-Up Activities And Exercises are geared toward students in grades 3-8. If modified, some of the Intermediate Warm-Up Activities And Exercises would be appropriate for primary students.

Chapter Four discusses nine mounts. Each mount is broken down into a step-by-step teaching approach covering the starting position, performance, and finishing position followed by specific teaching suggestions and spotting hints.

Chapter Five discusses nineteen stunts. Each stunt is broken down into a step-by-step teaching approach covering the starting position, performance, and finishing position followed by specific teaching suggestions and spotting hints.

Chapter Six discusses three turns. Each turn is broken down into a step-by-step teaching approach covering the starting position, performance, and finishing position followed by specific teaching suggestions and spotting hints.

Chapter Seven discusses five dismounts. Each dismount is broken down into a step-by-step teaching approach covering the starting position, performance, and finishing position followed by specific teaching suggestions and spotting hints.

Chapter Eight presents a Parallel Bars Progression Chart that you can use as a guide as to when to introduce the various parallel bars stunts, turns, mounts, and dismounts; however, do not feel compelled to accept the Chart as the final word.

Chapter Nine discusses examples of assessment in the three educational domains: psycho motor, cognitive, and affective. Assessment ideas are included for students at the primary level (grades K-2) and intermediate level (grades 3-8).

Chapter Ten discusses motivational ideas to reward student performance and effort. Motivational ideas are included for students at the primary level (grades K-2) and intermediate level (grades 3-8).

Finally, a Bibliography is included offering supplemental references to reinforce material presented in this book.

Chapter - 1

GENERAL TEACHING SUGGESTIONS

INTRODUCTION

The success of a progressive parallel bars unit through the grade levels is determined by the manner in which it is presented and the teacher's knowledge of the subject. The inclusion of a comprehensive gymnastics unit, which includes the parallel bars, is important to the child's overall learning experience.

Included in this Chapter are seventy-four General Teaching Suggestions to seriously consider when organizing your parallel bars unit. It is impossible to create the perfect instructional setting; however, every effort should be made to provide the best and most effective learning environment for the students.

Use and/or modify the following suggestions to fit your parallel bars unit. Because teaching styles and philosophies differ, you may wish to add to this list, or if necessary, delete certain suggestions.

GENERAL TEACHING SUGGESTIONS

1) Locate each set of parallel bars at a safe distance from walls and entrance ways.

2) Provide unobstructed and adequate pathways on all sides of the parallel bars.

3) Use a mat or mats to pad the area below and on both sides and ends of the parallel bars.

4) Provide adequate space for a waiting line.

5) Post the parallel bars rules near the parallel bars and make reference to them at appropriate times.

6) Supplement the parallel bars instruction with audiovisual aids, videos, loop films, etc.

7) Use parallel bars charts and related visual aids that meet the grade level, needs, and ability levels of the students.

8) Place the parallel bars charts and related visual aids on a wall close to the parallel bars or place the materials on a desk located at a safe distance from the parallel bars. Do not place teaching aids in locations where students travel.

9) Post important parallel bars vocabulary words on a wall close to the parallel bars to reinforce the learning experience and to supplement the school's reading program.

10) Develop a parallel bars collage by asking the students to draw and color pictures related to parallel bars stunts, turns, mounts, and dismounts.

11) Teach the parallel bars as a station within the total gymnastics and tumbling/fun stunts unit. Work with a small number of students, at one time, while the other students practice previously taught gymnastics and tumbling/fun stunts skills.

12) Develop a progressive parallel bars unit through the grade levels so learning is built upon previous learning experiences.

13) Develop a parallel bars unit for each class or grade level to fit the needs and ability levels of the students.

14) Make a class and/or grade level check sheet for all parallel bars stunts, turns, mounts, and dismounts. Check off skills covered on a daily basis.

15) Make the parallel bars stunt, turn, mount and dismount introduction and follow-up discussions concise and appropriate for the grade level and/or ability level of the students.

16) Teach the correct name of each parallel bars stunt, turn, mount, and dismount.

17) Use name cards or a chalkboard to reinforce the learning of the names of the parallel bars stunts, turns, mounts, and dismounts.

18) Review and reinforce key elements of previously taught parallel bars stunts, turns, mounts, and dismounts throughout the parallel bars/gymnastics unit.

19) Keep a record of students who are absent or unable to participate and during the next lesson be certain to cover the material which was missed during their absence.

20) Provide an introduction, summary, and follow-up within every lesson.

21) Include a warm-up session for each lesson to stretch muscles and body joints.

22) Discuss the need to have sufficient upper body and arm strength to be able to support the body on extended arms while both stationary and moving; as well as, to be able to maneuver the body below the bars.

23) Create a "Muscle Man" and/or "Muscle Woman" wall display to show the major muscle groups with the major muscle groups properly labeled. Discuss the major muscle groups used to support and move the body above and below the bars.

24) Remind the students of important parallel bars safety rules at the beginning of each lesson. Make the comments brief but effective.

25) Send a note or letter to parents explaining the importance of proper dress and footwear during the parallel bars/gymnastics unit.

26) Discuss the importance of wearing proper clothing and footwear. Cite specific examples.

27) Have students remove all objects from pockets and take off dangling jewelry, rings, hair combs, etc.

28) Discuss the importance of __not__ chewing gum or eating during the parallel/gymnastics unit.

29) Place your parallel bars teaching station in a location which allows you to observe all students at all supplemental gymnastics and tumbling/fun stunts areas.

30) Make certain all students are in positions which allow them to hear and observe all discussions and demonstrations.

31) Encourage a relaxed and somewhat quiet environment during the parallel bars/gymnastics unit. Discourage loud or sudden noises.

32) Emphasize controlled, deliberate movement for each stunt, turn, mount, and dismount.

33) Check the parallel bars on a daily basis to make certain the equipment is in proper working order to insure student safety.

34) Have the students tell you if the parallel bars are damaged or parts are loose.

35) Limit the number of students using the parallel bars at one time. The safest number is one; however, depending upon the age level and/or skills being performed, it could be safe to have two students using the parallel bars at the same time.

36) Discourage a waiting line. Instead, have each student perform one or two skills then dismount so more students are able to use the parallel bars within a specific time period.

37) Provide the best stunt, turn, mount, or dismount demonstration possible either by yourself or by an experienced student.

38) Always follow a demonstration with a brief discussion.

39) Give students opportunities to contribute ideas during the parallel bars class discussions. Encourage the students to share their feelings about the parallel bars activities.

40) Teach proper landing technique. Stress landing softly on the balls of the feet with the knees bent and head level.

41) Adjust the height and width of the parallel bars to meet the needs and ability levels of the students according to their ages and/or sizes.

42) Save time within each class period or provide time at the end of each class period to give students an opportunity to demonstrate learned or improved parallel bars stunts, turns, mounts, or dismounts with their classmates. Encourage students to applaud the performances of their fellow classmates.

43) Make note of students in need of remedial practice and give them individual or small group assistance outside the class setting, if possible.

44) Develop a positive and fair way to assess each student's performance.

45) Stress the importance of being responsible for one's behavior during all parallel bars/gymnastics lessons.

46) Reinforce all safety rules and be fair and firm in disciplining students who violate the rules.

47) Use _extreme_ caution when allowing students the freedom to hang upside down without the use of their hands. If permission is given, make certain the student

extends his/her arms and hands downward to be able to catch himself/herself, if the student's legs slip off the bars.

48) <u>Do not</u> allow students to stand on the parallel bars.

49) Exercise discretion when using student helpers. Provide them with guidance by establishing an organized and safe outline for the setup and take-down of the mat or mats under and around the parallel bars. Use extreme caution when allowing the students to assist with the transportation and movement of the parallel bars.

50) Use student spotters with caution. Be certain each spotter is capable of handling the responsibility. Take time to instruct the spotters in proper spotting techniques and continually monitor each spotter's performance.

51) Use adult volunteers to assist in spotting. Take time to instruct the adults in proper technique and continually monitor their performance.

52) Make certain proper spotting technique is used for each stunt, turn, mount, and dismount. Refer to the spotting hint section for each stunt, turn, mount, and dismount for proper clarification and explanation.

53) Give the students the responsibility of helping to keep the mat or mats beneath and around the parallel bars to ensure safety at all times.

54) Help each student to understand and to accept his/her specific ability level.

55) Stress the importance of trying one's best and be sincere with your comments.

56) Praise all students regardless of skill level.

57) Respect individual differences and provide opportunities for all students to succeed. Encourage students to be supportive of other student's accomplishments.

58) <u>Do not</u> physically force a student to perform a stunt, turn, mount, or dismount if the student is fearful of the performance. Instead, have the student perform a modified version of the stunt, turn, mount, or dismount, assuming the student is willing to do it. Help the student develop his/her self-confidence in a positive way.

59) Modify each stunt, turn, mount, or dismount to meet the ability level of each student according to body weight, experience, physical limitations, etc.

60) Praise students who display courtesy and compassion toward fellow classmates.

61) Capitalize on reciprocal teaching by having students assist one another when learning and performing parallel bars stunts, turns, mounts, and dismounts through the use of charts.

62) Show the students you are proud of their accomplishments and efforts by creating parallel bars achievement clubs. Give a certificate to each student who meets the standards for making a club.

63) Give the intermediate level students a written test at the end of the parallel bars/gymnastics unit to help assess their knowledge and understanding of the

material which was covered. The test results can be used as part of the student's grade for the parallel bars/gymnastics unit.

64) Discuss the word "routine" and have intermediate level students create their own parallel bars routines. Each routine should include a mount, stunts above and below the bars, a turn, and a dismount.

65) Give willing students opportunities to share their parallel bars routines with classmates. Encourage students to applaud the performances of their fellow classmates.

66) Create a variety of parallel bars routines from simple to complex and challenge the students to perform as many as possible. Encourage reciprocal teaching among the students.

67) Teach the three basic grips at the beginning of the parallel bars/gymnastics unit; overhand grip, underhand grip, and mixed grip.

68) Ask each student to draw a picture of himself or herself performing a stunt, turn, mount, or dismount and post the pictures throughout the gymnasium and hallways.

69) Encourage the classroom teachers to drop in during the parallel bars/gymnastics unit to observe and offer encouragement to the students.

70) Support the classroom language arts program by asking the classroom teacher to include a writing lesson centered around the student's parallel bars experience in physical education class.

71) Share and distribute available information and material for out-of-school instructional gymnastic programs.

72) Invite out-of-school gymnastics teams or troops to perform for students, teachers, and parents.

73) End the parallel bars/gymnastic unit by presenting an informal camera night program to parents, relatives, and friends. Give each grade level 30-45 minutes to share what they learned in class. Encourage the spectators to take pictures of the students performing their parallel bars/gymnastics skills.

74) Use the Parallel Bars Progression Chart on pages 132 and 133 as a reference for the inclusion of parallel bars stunts, turns, mounts, and dismounts throughout the grade levels.

Chapter - 2

GENERAL SAFETY RULES

INTRODUCTION

Generally, students of all ages and ability levels enjoy the challenges and opportunities presented within a well planned and organized parallel bars/gymnastics program. For most students, the parallel bars/gymnastics program experiences provided in the school's physical education program are the only experiences they receive. The vast majority of families do not have the financial resources to send their children to out-of-school gymnastics programs. Also, many families are geographically handicapped in that gymnastics programs are not within walking or driving distance of their homes. Thus, we, as physical educators, have the responsibility to provide a well rounded and sequential parallel bars/gymnastics program for all students. In so doing, we must set safety as our number one priority to ensure an enjoyable and safe learning experience for our students.

This Chapter includes fifty-four General Safety Rules to seriously consider before organizing and beginning your parallel bars unit. It is virtually impossible to eliminate all accidents in a physical education gymnastics program; however, every available precaution must be taken to help provide a safe learning environment for all students.

Use and/or modify the following rules to best fit your parallel bars unit. Because teaching styles and philosophies differ, you may wish to add to this list those rules you have found necessary and important in providing a safe parallel bars unit for your students.

GENERAL SAFETY RULES

1) Permit the use of the parallel bars, mats, and other pieces of gymnastics equipment __only__ when the gymnasium is supervised by a competent adult who has been trained in gymnastics. When the gymnasium is not being used, lock it securely in order to keep students and other persons away from the mats and pieces of gymnastics equipment.

2) Locate each set of parallel bars at a safe distance from walls, entrance ways, and other pieces of gymnastics equipment.

3) Provide unobstructed and adequate pathways on all sides of the parallel bars.

4) Use a mat or mats to pad the area below and on both sides and ends of the parallel bars.

5) Check the parallel bars on a daily basis to make certain they are in proper working order to ensure student safety.

6) Adjust the height and width of the parallel bars to meet the needs and ability levels of the students according to their ages and/or sizes.

7) Post the parallel bars rules near the parallel bars and make reference to them at appropriate times.

8) Use parallel bars charts and related visual aids that meet the grade levels, needs, and ability levels of the students. Do not provide materials that are beyond the capabilities of the students unless special provisions are made for their use. If some charts and related visual aids contain semi-advanced stunts/skills that meet the needs of a select group of students, make certain that all other students understand that these stunts/skills are to be performed by students who were given special permission. It is recommended to print "SPECIAL PERMISSION REQUIRED" next to these stunts/skills.

9) Place the parallel bars charts and related visual aids on a wall close to the parallel bars or place the materials on a desk located at a safe distance from the parallel bars. Do not place teaching aids in locations where students travel.

10) Develop a progressive parallel bars unit through the grade levels so learning is built upon previous learning experiences.

11) Teach the parallel bars stunts, turns, mounts, and dismounts in a progressive sequence according to their difficulty, if necessary.

12) Understand the stunts, turns, mounts, and dismounts to be taught and be able to break them down into teachable elements.

13) Emphasize the important safety precautions of each stunt, turn, mount, and dismount in relationship to proper hand placement/grip, appropriate body position or body parts positions, proper body weight placement to help with balance while being stationary and moving, amount of swing required to perform a specific skill, etc.

14) Use a daily lesson plan for each class and record the progress to maintain a continual check list of stunts, turns, mounts, and dismounts taught to the students.

15) Keep a record of students who were absent or unable to participate and during the next lesson be certain to cover the material which was missed during their absence.

16) Develop a parallel bars unit for each class or grade level to fit the needs and ability levels of the students.

17) Place your parallel bars teaching station in a location which will allow you to observe all students at all additional gymnastics and tumbling/fun stunts stations.

18) Always provide an adequate warm-up session at the beginning of the lesson to stretch muscles and body joints.

19) Review important parallel bars/gymnastics information and rules at the beginning of each lesson.

20) Encourage students to wear loose fitting and comfortable clothing and/or permit tights and leotards for ultimate comfort, safety, and maximum performance.

21) Stress the importance of performing in proper footwear. Encourage students to wear sneakers, tennis shoes, gymnastic slippers, or perform in bare feet. Check with local school administration and/or Board of Education policy before giving students permission to participate in bare feet. Do not permit a student to perform in stocking feet. (Stocking feet are very slippery!)

22) Have students remove all objects from pockets and take off dangling jewelry, rings, hair combs, etc.

23) Stress the importance of _not_ chewing gum or eating while engaged in parallel bars/gymnastics experiences.

24) Have the students wait their turn by standing a safe distance away from the parallel bars and performer.

25) Limit the number of students using the parallel bars at one time. The safest number is one; however, depending upon the age level and/or skill being performed, it could be safe to have two students using the parallel bars at the same time.

26) Stress the proper landing technique. Encourage landing softly on the balls of the feet with the knees bent and head level.

27) Have the students learn and use the correct grips for all stunts, turns, mounts, and dismounts.

28) Emphasize the importance of being a responsible student by listening carefully to the parallel bars instructions, rules, and directions.

29) Stress the importance of being responsible for one's behavior during all parallel bars/gymnastics lessons.

30) Omit any student for a predetermined period of time who violates the parallel bars/gymnastics safety rules. Be _fair,_.....but _firm_. Keep the safety of each student the number one priority.

31) Control the tempo of the lesson so students do not become fatigued. Stop the lesson periodically to review procedures, discuss key elements of specific lesson components and/or student responsibilities, and give students opportunities to demonstrate or discuss related material.

32) Encourage a relaxed and somewhat quiet environment during the parallel bars/-gymnastics unit. Discourage loud or sudden noises.

33) Always provide a demonstration of the proper execution of each stunt, turn, mount, or dismount by yourself, a skilled student, and/or an audiovisual aid during the introduction of a skill. Continue to provide demonstrations periodically throughout the learning experience.

34) Stress the important elements of a stunt, turn, mount, or dismount which are required to make the skill a safe one.

35) Emphasize controlled, deliberate movement for each stunt, turn, mount, and dismount to encourage safe, quality performance.

36) Spot each student through a specific stunt, turn, mount, or dismount prior to giving the student permission to do it by himself or herself, if necessary.

37) _Do not_ physically force a student to perform a stunt, turn, mount, or dismount if the student is fearful of the performance. Instead, have the student perform a modified version of the stunt, turn, mount, or dismount assuming the student is willing to do it. Help the student develop his/her self confidence in a positive way.

38) Modify each stunt, turn, mount, or dismount to meet the ability level of each student according to body weight, experience, physical limitations, etc., if necessary.

39) Carefully monitor students who are fearful, overweight, physically limited, or who lack the needed upper body and arm strength to perform the skills safely. Make a professional judgement, if it is absolutely necessary to restrict a student from attempting to perform a specific skill or group of skills that could put the student in unsafe situations. Talk to each student who might be in this category on a one to one basis. Be honest with the student. Tell the student which skills are safe for him/her to perform without your assistance or the assistance of a trained spotter. Be fair and above all....be careful. Make safety your number one priority!

40) Use extreme caution when allowing students the freedom to hang upside down without the use of the hands. If permission is given, make certain the student extends his/her arms and hands downward to be able to catch himself/herself in the event that the student's legs slip off the bar.

41) Do not allow students to stand on the parallel bars.

42) Exercise discretion when using student helpers. Provide them with guidance by establishing an organized and safe outline for the setup and take-down of the mat or mats under and around the parallel bars. Use extreme caution when allowing the students to assist with the transportation and movement of the parallel bars.

43) Permit spotting by persons who are totally responsible and who have been properly trained. Monitor the spotters closely and carefully.

44) Discourage student spotters. Encourage the students to rely upon their own performances.

45) Make certain you or any teacher designated spotter understands and uses the proper bodily position while spotting.

46) Encourage the students to help keep the mat or mats in correct position(s) beneath and around the parallel bars to ensure safety at all times.

47) Help each student understand and accept his/her ability level while performing on the parallel bars.

48) Encourage students to become accepting and tolerant of others and discourage students from ridiculing the attempts or mistakes of others.

49) Give advanced skill level students the opportunity to progress beyond the beginner/intermediate skill levels of other students; however, be certain all students understand and accept the exceptional skill level of these students. Share with all students the importance of progressing at one's personal ability level.

50) Create a learning environment in which the students understand that it is all right to ask for help.

51) Encourage the students to ask for assistance, if caught in an unsafe situation.

52) Encourage each student to tell you when an injury occurs, whether it is minor or serious.

53) Follow the school policy concerning the reporting of injuries.

54) Use discretion in assisting students who appear to have a serious injury. Send for the school nurse when in doubt.

Chapter - 3

WARM-UP ACTIVITIES AND EXERCISES

INTRODUCTION

In order for a child to be successful on the parallel bars, the child must have sufficient upper body and arm strength and abdominal strength. Upper body and arm strength are needed to support the body above the bars; as well as, maneuver the body below the bars. Abdominal strength is needed to allow controlled movement within the midsection of the body since many stunts, turns, mounts, and dismounts require bending at the waist.

This Chapter contains twenty-four primary level and intermediate level Warm-Up Activities and Exercises to help develop upper body and arm strength and abdominal strength. The primary level Activities are appropriate for students in grade two and below and the intermediate level Activities and Exercises are appropriate for students in grade three through eight. In addition, a General Warm-Up Routine is included that emphasizes bending and stretching movements. The routine is geared toward students in grade three through eight; however, if modified, the routine could easily be performed by students below grade three.

Every parallel bars/gymnastics lesson should start with a warm-up session. Begin the warm-up session with a one or two minute aerobic activity. Use a contemporary song for background music which has a tempo suitable for the selected aerobic activity. Then, follow with the General Warm-Up Routine. End the warm-up session by having the students perform Activities and/or Exercises to help develop upper body and arm strength and abdominal strength. Select two or three of the Activities and/or Exercises included within this chapter. Make certain you select at least one Activity or Exercise to help develop upper body and arm strength and at least one Activity or Exercise to help develop abdominal strength. The entire warm-up session should last between six and eight minutes.

PRIMARY WARM-UP ACTIVITIES

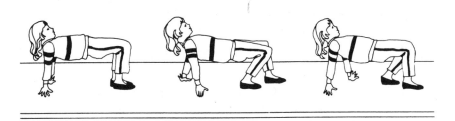

CRAB WALK FORWARD

STARTING POSITION
Assume a forward squatting position on the mat or in an open space on the floor. Reach back to place both hands on the mat or floor without sitting down. Separate the hands from the feet until the body (knees to shoulders) is parallel to the mat or floor, then lift the head. The hands are a shoulder-width apart with the hands and fingers pointed sideward. The legs and feet are slightly apart.

PERFORMANCE
Walk forward using the hands and feet to move the body. The hands and feet work
in opposition. Step forward with one hand while stepping forward with the opposite
foot then, without stopping, step forward with the other hand and foot while maintaining the proper body alignment. Continue to perform the Crab Walk Forward while
staying on the mat or traveling across an open space of floor.

FINISHING POSITION
End in a crab position on the mat or in an open space on the floor with the body being
supported by the hands and feet. The body (knees to shoulders) is parallel to the mat
or floor with the head lifted. The hands are a shoulder-width apart with the hands
and fingers pointed sideward. The legs and feet are slightly apart.

IMPORTANT TEACHING SUGGESTIONS

1) Take time in the introductory lesson to discuss the mechanics of the Crab Walk
Forward and follow up with a demonstration of the stunt by yourself or by
a skilled student. If possible, reinforce the discussion and demonstration with
a Crab Walk Forward chart and/or a related audiovisual aid.

2) Take time in the introductory lesson to individually assess the proper starting
position for each student and make necessary changes.

3) Emphasize the importance of keeping the body (knees to shoulders) parallel
to the mat or floor and not allowing the hips to drop. The body (knees to shoulders) must be kept in a straight line.

4) Discuss how the body resembles a crab. The arms and legs represent the crab's
legs and the body represents the crab's shell.

5) Challenge the students to "touch their tummies to the ceiling" to reinforce
the necessity to keep the hips high.

6) Use the teaching cue "lead with the feet" to help the students understand the
concept of the crab walking forward.

7) As a variation have the students perform the Crab Walk Forward using the hands
and feet in direct relationship with each other. Step forward on the hand and
foot on the same side of the body then use the other hand and foot while maintaining the proper body alignment.

8) As a modification ask the students to be a crab with a lame leg. Perform the
Crab Walk Forward with one hand or one foot off the mat or floor.

9) In order to make the experience more enjoyable and challenging, have the students perform the Crab Walk Forward for a certain distance. Then, stop and
lift one hand and the opposite foot and balance for five to ten seconds. Upon
completion, return the hand and foot to the mat or floor and continue to walk.

10) If appropriate, encourage the students to follow-up by practicing/performing
the Crab Walk Forward away from the school setting. Make certain the students
understand the need to practice/perform the Crab Walk Forward in a safe and
open space.

11) Ask the students in follow-up lessons whether or not they practiced/performed

the Crab Walk Forward away from the school setting. Commend the students who did their "homework" for being responsible and conscientious.

12) Assist students, if necessary.

CRAB WALK BACKWARD

STARTING POSITION
Assume a backward squatting position on the mat or in an open space on the floor. Reach back to place both hands on the mat or floor without sitting down. Separate the hands from the feet until the body (knees to shoulders) is parallel to the mat or floor, then left the head. The hands are a shoulder-width apart with the hands and fingers pointed sideward. The legs and feet are slightly apart.

PERFORMANCE
Walk backward using the hands and feet to move the body. The hands and feet work in opposition. Step backward with one hand while stepping backward with the opposite foot then, without stopping, step backward with the other hand and foot while maintaining the proper body alignment. Continue to perform the Crab Walk Backward while staying on the mat or traveling across an open space of floor.

FINISHING POSITION
End in a crab position on the mat or in an open space on the floor with the body being supported by the hands and feet. The body (knees to shoulders) is parallel to the mat or floor with the head lifted. The hands are a shoulder-width apart with the hands and fingers pointed sideward. The legs and feet are slightly apart.

IMPORTANT TEACHING SUGGESTIONS

1) Take time in the introductory lesson to discuss the mechanics of the Crab Walk Backward and follow up with a demonstration of the stunt by yourself or by a skilled student. If possible, reinforce the discussion and demonstration with a Crab Walk Backward chart and/or a related audio visual aid.

2) Take time in the introductory lesson to individually assess the proper starting position for each student and make necessary changes.

3) Emphasize the importance of keeping the body (knees to shoulders) parallel to the mat or floor and _not_ allowing the hips to drop. The body (knees to shoulders) _must_ be kept in a straight line.

4) Discuss how the body resembles a crab. The arms and legs represent the crab's legs and the body represents the crab's shell.

5) Challenge the students to "touch their tummies to the ceiling" to reinforce the necessity to keep the hips high.

6) Use the teaching cue "lead with the hands" to help the students understand the concept of the crab walking backward.

7) As a variation have the students perform the Crab Walk Backward using the hands and feet in direct relationship with each other. Step backward on the hand and foot on the same side of the body then use the other hand and foot while maintaining the proper body alignment.

8) As a modification ask the students to be a crab with a lame leg. Perform the Crab Walk Backward with one hand or one foot off the mat or floor.

9) In order to make the experience more enjoyable and challenging, have the students perform the Crab Walk Backward for a certain distance. Then, stop and lift one hand and the opposite foot and balance for five to ten seconds. Upon completion, return the hand and foot to the mat or floor and continue to walk.

10) If appropriate, encourage the students to follow-up by practicing/performing the Crab Walk Backward away from the school setting. Make certain the students understand the need to practice/perform the Crab Walk Backward in a safe and open space.

11) Ask the students in follow-up lessons whether or not they practiced/performed the Crab Walk Backward away from the school setting. Commend the students who did their "homework" for being responsible and conscientious.

12) Assist students, if necessary.

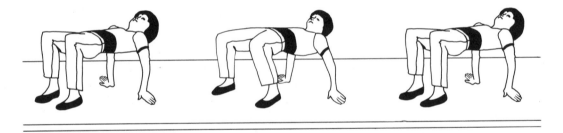

CRAB WALK SIDEWARD

STARTING POSITION
Assume a sideward squatting position on the mat or in an open space on the floor. Reach back to place both hands on the mat or floor without sitting down. Separate the hands from the feet until the body (knees to shoulders) is parallel to the mat or floor, then lift the head. The hands are a shoulder-width apart with the hands and fingers pointed sideward. The legs and feet are slightly apart.

PERFORMANCE
Walk sideward using the hands and feet to move the body. The hands and feet work in direct relationship with each other. Step sideward with the hand and foot on the same side of the body then use the other hand and foot while maintaining the proper body alignment. Continue to perform the Crab Walk Sideward while staying on the mat or traveling across an open space of floor.

FINISHING POSITION
End in a crab position on the mat or in an open space on the floor with the body being supported by the hands and feet. The body (knees to shoulders) is parallel to the mat or floor with the head lifted. The hands are a shoulder-width apart with the hands and fingers pointed sideward. The legs and feet are slightly apart.

IMPORTANT TEACHING SUGGESTIONS

1) Take time in the introductory lesson to discuss the mechanics of the Crab Walk Sideward and follow up with a demonstration of the stunt by yourself or by a skilled student. If possible, reinforce the discussion and demonstration with a Crab Walk Sideward chart and/or a related audio visual aid.

2) Take time in the introductory lesson to individually assess the proper starting position for each student and make necessary changes.

3) Emphasize the importance of keeping the body (knees to shoulders) parallel to the mat or floor and _not_ allowing the hips to drop. The body (knees to shoulders) _must_ be kept in a straight line.

4) Discuss how the body resembles a crab. The arms and legs represent the crab's legs and the body represents the crab's shell.

5) Challenge the students to "touch their tummies to the ceiling" to reinforce the necessity to keep the hips high.

6) Use the teaching cue "lead with the hand and foot" to help the students understand the concept of the crab walking sideward.

7) As a variation have the students perform the Crab Walk Sideward using the hands and feet in opposition of each other. Step sideward with one hand while stepping sideward with the opposite foot. Then, without stopping, step sideward with the other hand and foot while maintaining the proper body alignment.

8) As a modification ask the students to be a crab with a lame leg. Perform the Crab Walk Sideward with one hand or one foot off the mat or floor.

9) In order to make the experience more enjoyable and challenging, have the students perform the Crab Walk Sideward for a certain distance. Then, stop and lift one hand and the opposite foot and balance for five to ten seconds. Upon completion, return the hand and foot to the mat or floor and continue to walk.

10) If appropriate, encourage the students to follow-up by practicing/performing the Crab Walk Sideward away from the school setting. Make certain the students understand the need to practice/perform the Crab Walk Sideward in a safe and open space.

11) Ask the students in follow-up lessons whether or not they practiced/performed the Crab Walk Sideward away from the school setting. Commend the students who did their "homework" for being responsible and conscientious.

12) Assist students, if necessary.

CRAB KICKS

STARTING POSITION
Assume a forward squatting position on the mat or in an open space on the floor. Reach back to place both hands on the mat or floor without sitting down. Separate the hands from the feet until the body (knees to shoulders) is parallel to the mat or floor, then lift the head. The hands are a shoulder-width apart with the hands and fingers pointed sideward. The legs and feet are slightly apart.

PERFORMANCE
While keeping the body in the proper crab position on the mat or floor, lift and kick one leg and foot then lower the leg and return the foot to its original position on the mat or floor. Next, lift and kick the other leg and foot then lower the leg and return the foot to its original position on the mat or floor. Continue to perform the Crab Kicks a minimum of five times.

FINISHING POSITION
End in a crab position on the mat or in an open space on the floor with the body being supported by the hands and feet. The body (knees to shoulders) is parallel to the mat or floor with the head lifted. The hands are a shoulder-width apart with the hands and fingers pointed sideward. The legs and feet are slightly apart.

IMPORTANT TEACHING SUGGESTIONS

1) Take time in the introductory lesson to discuss the mechanics of the Crab Kicks and follow-up with a demonstration of the stunt by yourself or by a skilled student.

2) Take time in the introductory lesson to individually assess the proper starting position for each student and make necessary changes.

3) Emphasize the importance of keeping the body (knees to shoulders) parallel to the mat or floor and not allowing the hips to drop. The body (knees to shoulders) must be kept in a straight line.

4) Discuss how the body resembles a crab. The arms and legs represent the crab's legs and the body represents the crab's shell.

5) Challenge the students to "touch their tummies to the ceiling" to reinforce the necessity to keep the hips high.

6) Challenge the students to "kick their feet to touch the ceiling" to reinforce the need to kick the feet as high as possible.

7) As a modification, ask the students to perform the Crab Kicks while traveling in a Crab Walk Forward position (refer to pages 13 & 14 for teaching guidelines), Crab Walk Backward (refer to page 15 for teaching guidelines), or Crab Walk Sideward (refer to page 16 for teaching guidelines).

8) If appropriate, encourage the students to follow-up by practicing/performing the Crab Kicks away from the school setting. Make certain the students understand the need to practice/perform the Crab Kicks in a safe and open space.

9) Ask the students in follow-up lessons whether or not they practiced/performed the Crab Kicks away from the school setting. Commend the students who did their "homework" for being responsible and conscientious.

10) Assist students, if necessary.

BEAR WALK

STARTING POSITION
Assume a bent at the waist forward balancing position with the feet and hands on a mat or in an open space on the floor. The legs are straight with the feet slightly apart and pointed forward. The arms are locked with the hands positioned directly below the shoulders, and the fingers are slightly apart and pointed forward. The head is lifted with the eyes focused on the mat or floor in front of the hands.

PERFORMANCE
The hands and feet work in direct relationship with each other. Walk forward on the hand and foot on the same side of the body then use the other hand and foot while maintaining the proper bent at the waist straight legs and locked arms body position. Keep the head lifted with the eyes focused on the mat or floor in front of the hands throughout the performance of the Bear Walk. Continue to perform the Bear Walk while staying on the mat or traveling across an open space of floor.

FINISHING POSITION
End in a bent at the waist forward balancing position with the feet and hands on a mat or in an open space on the floor. The legs are straight with the feet slightly apart and pointed forward. The arms are locked with the hands positioned directly below the shoulders, and the fingers are slightly apart and positioned forward. The head is lifted with the eyes focused on the mat or floor in front of the hands.

IMPORTANT TEACHING SUGGESTIONS

1) Take time in the introductory lesson to discuss the mechanics of the Bear Walk and follow-up with a demonstration of the stunt by yourself or by a skilled student. If possible, reinforce the discussion and demonstration with a Bear Walk chart and/or a related audiovisual aid.

2) Take time in the introductory lesson to individually assess the proper starting position for each student.

3) Encourage the students to walk with the legs straight and the arms locked; however, allow for a slight bend in the knees, if necessary.

4) Tell the students to keep the head lifted with the eyes focused on the mat or floor in front of the hands.

5) Discuss how the body resembles a bear. The arms and hands represent the bear's front legs and paws, and the legs and feet represent the bear's back legs and paws.

6) Encourage the students to growl like a bear as they walk across the mat or floor.

7) Ask the students to pretend to be a bear walking across the field in search of food.

8) As a variation have the students perform the Bear Walk by moving the legs and arms in opposition. Walk forward with one hand while stepping forward with the opposite foot then, without stopping, step forward with the other hand and foot while maintaining the proper bent at the waist straight legs and locked arms position.

9) As a variation have the students perform the Bear Walk for a predetermined distance or length of time, then without stopping or changing the body position on the mat or floor, reverse the Bear Walk. Walk backward on the hand and foot on the same side of the body then use the other hand and foot while maintaining the proper bent at the waist straight legs and locked arms body position.

10) If appropriate, encourage the students to follow-up by practicing/performing the Bear Walk away from the school setting. Make certain the students understand the need to practice/perform the Bear Walk in a safe and open space.

11) Ask the students in follow-up lessons whether or not they practiced/performed the Bear Walk away from the school setting. Commend the students who did their "homework" for being responsible and conscientious.

12) Assist students, if necessary.

TURTLE WALKER

STARTING POSITION
Assume a modified prone position on a mat or in an open space on the floor. The arms are slightly bent with the hands directly below the shoulders. The fingers are pointed forward. The feet are spread apart. The head is lifted with the eyes focused forward. The body is being supported by the shoulders, arms, and hands with the toes touching the mat or floor.

PERFORMANCE
Travel forward using the hands and feet to move the body. The hands and feet work in direct relationship with each other. Step forward on the hand and foot on the same side of the body then use the other hand and foot while maintaining the proper modified prone position. Continue to perform the Turtle Walker while staying on the mat or traveling across an open space of floor.

FINISHING POSITION
End in a modified prone position on a mat or in an open space on the floor. The arms are slightly bent with the hands directly below the shoulders. The fingers are pointed forward. The feet are spread apart. The head is lifted with the eyes focused forward. The body is being supported by the shoulders, arms, and hands with the toes touching the mat or floor.

IMPORTANT TEACHING SUGGESTIONS

1) Take time in the introductory lesson to discuss the mechanics of the Turtle Walker and follow-up with a demonstration of the stunt by yourself or by a skilled student.

2) Take time in the introductory lesson to individually assess the proper starting position for each student.

3) Encourage the students to bend the knees slightly as they perform the Turtle Walker.

4) Emphasize the importance of keeping the body parallel to the mat or floor and not allowing the hips to drop to create a valley or allowing the hips to rise to create a mountain.

5) Have the students begin by taking small steps then challenge the students to increase the size of the steps as they become stronger and more confident.

6) Discuss how the body resembles a turtle. The arms and legs represent the turtle's legs and the body represents the turtle's shell.

7) Challenge the advanced/stronger students to perform the Turtle Walker by widening the distance between the hands and between the feet. The wider distance between the hands and between the feet causes greater stress on the muscles, however do not allow the separation to be so great that it becomes unsafe.

8) Discuss the need to have sufficient strength in the upper body and arms to perform the Turtle Walker correctly and safely. Also, discuss the need to have adequate strength within the midsection of the body to keep the body straight throughout the performance of the Turtle Walker.

9) As a variation have the students perform the Turtle Walker using the hands and feet in opposition with each other. Step forward with one hand while stepping forward with the opposite foot. Then, without stopping, step forward with the other hand and foot while maintaining the proper body alignment.

10) As a variation have the students perform the Turtle Walker for a predetermined distance or length of time, then without stopping or changing the body position on the mat or floor, reverse the Turtle Walker. Walk backward using the hands and feet to propel the body.

11) As a variation have the students perform the Turtle Walker while traveling sideward on the mat or across an open space of floor. The hands and feet work in direct relationship with each other. Step sideward with the hand and foot on the same side of the body then use the other hand and foot while maintaining the proper body alignment.

12) If appropriate, encourage the students to follow-up by practicing/performing the Turtle Walker away from the school setting. Make certain the students understand the need to practice/perform the Turtle Walker in a safe and open space.

13) Ask the students in follow-up lessons whether or not they practiced/performed the Turtle Walker away from the school setting. Commend the students who did their "homework" for being responsible and conscientious.

14) Assist students, if necessary.

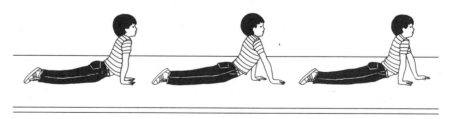

SEAL WALK

STARTING POSITION
Assume a modified front leaning rest position on a mat or in an open space on the floor with the upper body being supported on straightened arms. The legs are together

and straight with the toes pointed backward. The hands are a shoulder-width apart with the fingers pointed forward or sideward. The head is level with the eyes focused forward.

PERFORMANCE
Walk forward on the hands with the arms straight while dragging the legs and feet across the mat or floor. Keep the head level and the legs together and straight with the toes pointed backward. Continue to perform the Seal Walk while staying on the mat or traveling across an open space of floor.

FINISHING POSITION
End in a modified front leaning rest position on a mat or in an open space on the floor with the upper body being supported on straightened arms. The legs are together and straight with the toes pointed backward. The hands are a shoulder-width apart with the fingers pointed forward or sideward. The head is level with eyes focused forward.

IMPORTANT TEACHING SUGGESTIONS

1) Take time in the introductory lesson to discuss the mechanics of the Seal Walk and follow-up with a demonstration of the stunt by yourself or by a skilled student. If possible, reinforce the discussion and demonstration with a Seal Walk chart and/or a related audiovisual aid.

2) Take time in the introductory lesson to individually assess the proper starting position for each student.

3) Emphasize the importance of keeping the arms straight and the legs together and straight with the toes pointed backward throughout the performance of the Seal Walk.

4) Stress the necessity of pulling with the arms and hands in order to drag the lower body across the mat or floor.

5) Discuss how the body resembles a seal. The arms and hands represent the seal's flippers and the legs and feet represent the seal's tail.

6) Encourage the students to bark like a seal as they travel across the mat or floor.

7) As a variation have the students perform the Seal Walk for a predetermined distance or length of time, then without stopping or changing the body position on the mat or floor, reverse the Seal Walk. Walk backward on the hands while pushing the lower body.

8) As a variation have the students perform the Seal Walk with the hands and fingers pointed in a backward direction.

9) As a modification for students who are overweight or students with lower arm and/or hand limitations, have them perform the Seal Walk using the elbows instead of the hands to propel the body across the mat. Do not allow these students to perform this modification on the floor.

10) In order to make the experience more enjoyable for the students, have them perform the Seal Walk for a predetermined distance or length of time, then

roll over on the back and clap the hands (flippers) together while making seal sounds. Tell the students to be happy seals.

11) Relate the fun experience to a seal giving a performance and have the students perform the Seal Walk with the nose in the air to pretend to balance a ball on the nose.

12) If appropriate, encourage the students to follow-up by practicing/performing the Seal Walk away from the school setting. Make certain the students understand the need to practice/perform the Seal Walk in a safe and open space.

13) Ask the students in follow-up lessons whether or not they practiced/performed the Seal Walk away from the school setting. Commend the students who did their "homework" for being responsible and conscientious.

14) Assist students, if necessary.

INCHWORM

STARTING POSITION
Assume a front leaning rest (push-up) position on the mat or in an open space on the floor. The arms are locked and the hands are positioned directly below the shoulders with the fingers slightly apart and pointed forward. The legs are together with the toes touching the mat or floor. The head is lifted with the eyes focused on the mat or floor in front of the hands.

PERFORMANCE
Walk the feet toward the hands while keeping the legs together and straight to position the feet as close as possible to the hands. The head, shoulders, arms, and hands remain stationary. Continue to move forward by walking the hands away from the feet. The arms stay locked. The feet remain stationary with the legs straight and the legs and feet together. Throughout the performance of the Inchworm, allow the hips to bend to permit forward movement. Continue to perform the Inchworm while staying on the mat or traveling across an open space of floor.

FINISHING POSITION
End in a front leaning rest (push-up) position on the mat or in an open space on the floor. The arms are locked and the hands are positioned directly below the shoulders with the fingers slightly apart and pointed forward. The legs are together with the toes touching the mat or floor. The head is lifted with the eyes focused on the mat or floor in front of the hands.

IMPORTANT TEACHING SUGGESTIONS

1) Take time in the introductory lesson to discuss the mechanics of the Inchworm and follow-up with a demonstration of the stunt by yourself or by a skilled student. If possible, reinforce the discussion and demonstration with an Inchworm chart and/or a related audiovisual aid.

2) Take time in the introductory lesson to individually assess the proper starting position for each student and make necessary changes.

3) Emphasize the importance of keeping the arms locked and the legs together and straight throughout the performance of the Inchworm.

4) Encourage the students to keep the body straight from head to heels while performing the starting and finishing positions.

5) Discuss how the body resembles an Inchworm. The head, shoulders, arms and hands represent the front of the Inchworm, and the legs and feet represent the end of the Inchworm. The hips and buttocks represent the center of the Inchworm that goes up and down as the Inchworm travels along the mat or across the floor.

6) Use the teaching cue "<u>walk your feet forward to say 'Hi' to your hands</u>" when moving the feet toward the hands.

7) Use the teaching cue "<u>walk your hands forward and say 'Good-bye' to your feet</u>" when moving the hands away from the feet.

8) If appropriate, encourage the students to follow-up by practicing/performing the Inchworm away from the school setting. Make certain the students understand the need to practice/perform the Inchworm in a safe and open space.

9) Ask the students in follow-up lessons whether or not they practiced/performed the Inchworm away from the school setting. Commend the students who did their "homework" for being responsible and conscientious.

10) Assist students, if necessary.

COFFEE GRINDER

STARTING POSITION
Assume a left side leaning rest position on the middle of the mat or in an open space on the floor with the body supported by the left arm and hand. The left arm is locked with the fingers spread apart. The body is extended and straight with the outside of the left foot and the inside of the right foot touching the mat or floor. The right arm is resting on the right side of the body and the head is aligned with the body.

PERFORMANCE
Walk forward in a slow, controlled manner around the left hand to make a complete circle as the left hand turns in place. Keep the left arm locked and the body extended and straight. The right arm remains in a resting position on the right side of the body with the head aligned with the body.

FINISHING POSITION
End in a left side leaning rest position on the middle of the mat or in an open space on the floor with the body supported by the left arm and hand. The left arm is locked

with the fingers spread apart. The body is extended and straight with the outside of the left foot and the inside of the right foot touching the mat or floor. The right arm is resting on the right side of the body and the head is aligned with the body.

IMPORTANT TEACHING SUGGESTIONS

1) Take time in the introductory lesson to discuss the mechanics of the Coffee Grinder and follow-up with a demonstration of the stunt by yourself or by a skilled student. If possible, reinforce the discussion and demonstration with a Coffee Grinder chart and/or a related audiovisual aid.

2) Take time in the introductory lesson to individually assess the proper starting position for each student and make necessary changes.

3) Make certain the students practice and/or perform the Coffee Grinder on a mat or in a safe and open space on the floor. The space must be large enough to allow each student freedom of movement while traveling around the support arm and hand without the possibility of touching another student, piece of equipment, wall, etc.

4) Share the need to keep the left arm (support arm) locked and the fingers spread apart throughout the performance of the Coffee Grinder.

5) Stress the need to turn the hand on the mat or floor as the body moves around the hand.

6) Encourage the students to keep the body extended and straight throughout the performance of the Coffee Grinder.

7) Discuss the purpose of a Coffee Grinder and how it was used. Introduce the word antique and explain why a Coffee Grinder is considered an antique.

8) Discuss how the body represents the handle of a Coffee Grinder.

9) Use the teaching cue "keep the body as stiff as a handle" to reinforce the necessity for keeping the body extended and straight.

10) Ask the students to pretend to be Coffee Grinders grinding coffee beans. Make certain you explain coffee beans.

11) After the students travel around the left support arm and hand, have the students perform the Coffee Grinder by assuming a right side leaning rest position with the body being supported by the right arm and hand.

12) As a variation have the students perform the Coffee Grinder to make a complete forward circle, then without stopping or changing the body position on the mat or floor, reverse the Coffee Grinder. Walk backward in a slow, controlled manner around the hand as the hand turns in place. Then, perform the forward and backward Coffee Grinder with the body supported by the other arm and hand.

13) If appropriate, encourage the students to follow-up by practicing/performing the Coffee Grinder away from the school setting. Make certain the students understand the need to practice/perform the Coffee Grinder in a safe and open space.

14) Ask the students in follow-up lessons whether or not they practiced/performed the Coffee Grinder away from the school setting. Commend the students who did their "homework" for being responsible and conscientious.

15) Assist students, if necessary.

INTERMEDIATE WARM-UP ACTIVITIES AND EXERCISES

"FOLLOW THE LEADER" GENERAL WARM-UP ROUTINE

Young students enjoy participating in a follow the leader activity because it gives them an opportunity to create and/or imitate a variety of bodily movements. Organize and lead a follow the leader warm-up activity which takes all body parts and joints through an array of bending, stretching, twisting, turning, pushing, pulling, and swinging movements. Make the movements slow, deliberate, and meaningful. If possible, use background music to reinforce the movements, and to help establish the tempo and tone of the activity. Perform the activity for three to five minutes. Be certain each student participates in a safe and open space on the floor. Afterward, ask for student responses and/or feelings toward the experience.

Watch for students who excel in their movements and demonstrate creativity. Give these students opportunities to lead the class. During the student led sessions, move throughout the group to assist, correct, praise, and offer words of encouragement. Acknowledge the leaders and followers for a job well done, assuming they were on task.

EXERCISES

Including a variety of exercises, which emphasize bending and stretching movements, can be a challenging and beneficial way to warm-up students for a parallel bars/gymnastics lesson in grades three through eight. However, many of the exercises through modification can be successfully performed by students below grade three. Begin the "Exercises" warm-up session with a two or three minute aerobic activity; for example, jogging or running in place. Use a contemporary song for background music which has a tempo suitable for running in place. Then, follow with the exercises.

There are a wide range of exercises appropriate for use in a parallel bars/gymnastics warm-up session. Below are listed several exercises that start with the head and neck and work their way down to the ankles. Each exercise is listed separately and is accompanied by a descriptive drawing and explanation.

Start in a standing position with feet slightly apart, knees slightly bent, and arms beside the body in a relaxed position.

HEAD ROLL

Tilt head right: slowly roll head from right down and over to left: tuck chin to chest when the head is forward: repeat roll from left to right. Perform five times. <u>Do not</u> roll the head backward.

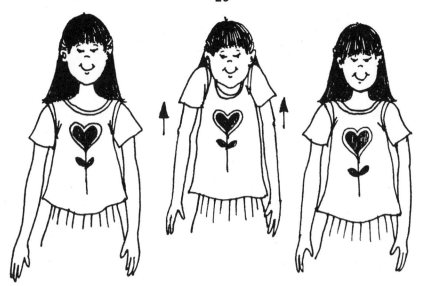

SHOULDER LIFTS

Start with shoulders in a relaxed position: lift (shrug) shoulders: relax shoulders to return to start position. Perform five times. Use a slow tempo of movement.

SHOULDER ROLLS: BACKWARD

Start with shoulders in a relaxed position: rotate both shoulders forward, upward, backward, and downward in a circular pattern. Perform five times. Use a slow tempo of movement.

SHOULDER ROLLS: FORWARD

Start with shoulders in a relaxed position: rotate both shoulders backward, upward, forward, and downward in a circular pattern. Perform five times. Use a slow tempo of movement.

ARM CIRCLES: BACKWARD LARGE CIRCLES

Start with arms extended sideward: circle arms backward to create large circles. Perform five times. Use a slow tempo of movement.

ARM CIRCLES: FORWARD LARGE CIRCLES

Start with arms extended sideward: circle arms forward to create large circles. Perform five times. Use a slow tempo of movement.

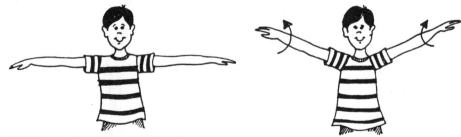

ARM CIRCLES: BACKWARD SMALL CIRCLES

Start with arms extended sideward: circle arms backward to create small cirlces. Perform five times. Use a slow tempo of movement.

ARM CIRCLES: FORWARD SMALL CIRCLES

Start with arms extended sideward: circle arms forward to create small circles. Perform five times. Use a slow tempo of movement.

OVERHEAD STRETCH AND REACH

Start with feet together, knees slightly bent, and arms beside body in relaxed position: reach upward with arms extended and fingers straight, legs locked, and balls of feet on floor: return to start position. Perform three times. Hold overhead stretch and reach position for 5 to 7 seconds.

SIDEWARD STRADDLE STRETCH AND REACH

Start with feet together, knees slightly bent, and arms beside body in relaxed position: reach sideward with arms extended and fingers straight, legs locked in straddle position, and feet flat on the floor: return to start position. Perform three times. Hold each sideward straddle stretch and reach position for 5 to 7 seconds.

SIDE BENDS: RIGHT

Start with feet a shoulder-width apart and toes pointed diagonally forward. The legs are slightly bent. The left arm is extended overhead with fingers pointed upward. The right arm is beside the body in a relaxed position. Bend slowly at the waist to the right keeping the left arm beside the head. Keep the hips in place. Take the right arm diagonally across in front of the body. Return to start position. Perform three times. Hold each side bend to right for 5 to 7 seconds.

SIDE BENDS: LEFT

Start with feet a shoulder-width apart and toes pointed diagonally forward. The legs are slightly bent. The right arm is extended overhead with fingers pointed upward. The left arm is beside the body in a relaxed position. Bend slowly at the waist to the left keeping the right arm beside the head. Keep the hips in place. Take the left arm diagonally across in front of the body. Return to the start position. Perform three times. Hold each side bend to the left for 5 to 7 seconds.

Variation: Alternate side bend right then left. Perform three times. Hold each side bend for 5 to 7 seconds.

BODY ROLL: RIGHT

Start with feet a shoulder-width apart and toes pointed diagonally forward. The legs are slightly bent. The hands are placed on the hips. Bend slowly at the waist to the right, backward, left, and forward. Keep the hips in place. Perform five times. Do not return to the start position after beginning the body rolls. Make the five body rolls continuous. Hold each position 2 to 3 seconds.

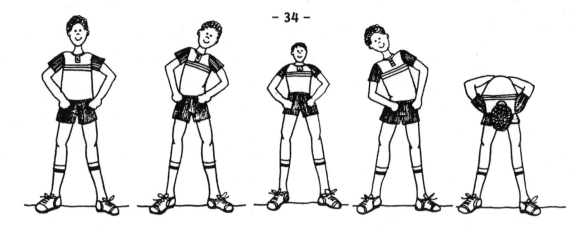

BODY ROLL: LEFT

Start with feet a shoulder-width apart and toes pointed diagonally forward. The legs are slightly bent. The hands are placed on the hips. Bend slowly at the waist to the left, backward, right, and forward. Keep the hips in place. Perform five times. <u>Do not</u> return to the start position after beginning the body rolls. Make the five body rolls continuous. Hold each bend position 2 to 3 seconds.

Variation: Alternate body rolls right then left. Perform five times. Hold each bend position 2 to 3 seconds.

TWISTERS

Start with feet a shoulder-width apart and toes pointed diagonally forward. The arms and fingers are extended sideward at shoulder level. Twist slowly to the right at the waist by extending the right arm backward as the left arm wraps across the chest. Keep the head in a stationary position with eyes focused forward. Return slowly to the start position. Twist slowly to the left at the waist by extending the left arm backward as the right arm wraps across the chest. Keep the head in a stationary position with eyes focused forward. Return slowly to the start position. Perform five times.

SEATED STRADDLE POSITION STRETCH

Sit on the floor with legs in a straddle position with the toes pointed. The back is straight with the head level. Slowly bend forward at the hips with the back straight to reach toward the ankles or toes. Initiate the stretch from the hips. Keep the chin in a neutral position: somewhere between being held upward or downward. This will keep the head and neck in a good position during the stretch. Keep shoulders and arms relaxed. Hold each seated straddle position stretch for 10 to 15 seconds. Return to the start position. Perform three times.

Variation: Do the seated straddle position stretch by reaching forward between the legs and feet. Hold each stretch for 10 to 15 seconds. Perform three times.

SEATED PIKE POSITION STRETCH

Sit on the floor with the legs together and straight with the toes pointed. The back is straight with the head level. Slowly bend forward at the hips with the back straight to reach toward the ankles or toes. Initiate the stretch from the hips. Keep the chin in a neutral position: somewhere between being held upward or downward. This will keep the head and neck in a good position during the stretch. Keep the shoulders and arms relaxed. Hold each seated pike position stretch for 10 to 15 seconds. Return to the start position. Perform three times.

FOOT CIRCLES: OUTWARD

Sit on the floor with legs bent and feet flat on the floor. Place the hands on the floor beside and slightly behind the hips. Lift feet off the floor to balance on the buttocks. Remain in a seated position. <u>Do not</u> lie back. Rotate both feet outward in a circular motion. Return to the start position. Perform five foot circles.

FOOT CIRCLES: INWARD

Sit on the floor with legs bent and feet flat on the floor. Place the hands on the floor beside and slightly behind the hips. Lift feet off the floor to balance on the buttocks. Remain in a seated position. <u>Do not</u> lie back. Rotate both feet inward in a circular motion. Return to the start position. Perform five foot circles.

Variation: Perform five outward foot circles immediately followed by five inward foot circles.

IMPORTANT REMINDERS FOR ALL EXERCISES AND ACTIVITIES

In the introductory lesson have each student find a safe and open space on the floor. Demonstrate and explain each exercise in full view of all students. Then ask the students to perform each exercise. Do one exercise at a time. Take time to visually assess and/or move throughout the group to reinforce the learning experience. Praise and encourage all student efforts and accomplishments, assuming the students are on task.

The follow-up warm-up sessions will progress much faster because the students will be more familiar with the exercises through repetition and practice. Continue to do the exercises individually or combine them together to create an exercise routine. If possible, use background music to reinforce the exercises. Select contemporary music that contains a tempo to fit the activity level of the exercises.

Watch for students who excel in their performances of the exercises. Give these students opportunities to lead the class. During the student lead sessions, move throughout the group to assist, praise, and offer words of encouragement. Acknowledge the leaders and followers for a job well done, assuming they were on task. The follow-up warm-up sessions should last approximately five to seven minutes.

PUSH-PULLER

STARTING POSITION
Assume a sitting position with the legs crossed on a mat or in an open space on the floor. The back is straight with the head level and the eyes focused forward. The arms are lifted with the hands positioned in front of the chest. The palms are together with the fingers interlocked.

PERFORMANCE
This is a two part exercise. In part one have the students push their hands together tightly for five seconds. Then, in part two have the students gently pull their hands apart while keeping the fingers interlocked for five seconds. Repeat parts one and two a minimum of three times.

FINISHING POSITION
End in a sitting position with the legs crossed on a mat or in an open space on the floor. The back is straight with the head level and the eyes focused forward. The arms are lifted with the hands positioned in front of the chest. The palms are together with the fingers interlocked.

IMPORTANT TEACHING SUGGESTIONS

1) Take time in the introductory lesson to discuss the mechanics of the Push-Puller and follow-up with a demonstration of the exercise by yourself or by a skilled student.

2) Take time in the introductory lesson to individually assess the proper starting position for each student.

3) Emphasize the importance of keeping the back straight and the arms lifted with the hands positioned in front of the chest throughout both phases of the exercise.

4) Discuss the difference between the two non-locomotor movements: push and pull.

5) Discuss the terms "isometric exercise" and "static exercise" and relate the terms to the performance of the Push-Puller.

6) Mention the major muscle groups in the upper body and arms that are used to perform the Push-Puller.

7) Increase the length of time to a maximum of ten seconds for each part of the exercise as the students become stronger and show proficiency while performing the Push-Puller.

8) If appropriate, encourage the students to follow-up by practicing/performing the Push-Puller away from the school setting. Make certain the students understand the need to practice/perform the Push-Puller in a safe and open space.

9) Ask the students in follow-up lessons whether or not they practiced/performed the Push-Puller away from the school setting. Commend the students who did their "homework" for being responsible and conscientious.

10) Assist students, if necessary.

UPPER BODY PUSH-UP

STARTING POSITION
Assume a straight leg sitting position with the legs together on the mat or in an open space on the floor. The arms are fully extended at the sides with the hands placed palms down beside the hips on the floor or on the mat. The fingers are pointed forward. The back is straight with the head level and the eyes focused forward.

PERFORMANCE
Push down on the hands to raise the body off the mat or off the floor. The heels remain in contact with the mat or floor. Slowly and carefully lower the body to return to the starting position. Keep the back and legs straight. Continue to perform the Upper Body Push-Up a minimum of five times.

FINISHING POSITION
End in a straight leg sitting position with the legs together on the mat or in an open space on the floor. The arms are fully extended at the sides with the hands placed palms down beside the hips on the floor or on the mat. The fingers are pointed forward. The back is straight with the head level and the eyes focused forward.

IMPORTANT TEACHING SUGGESTIONS

1) Take time in the introductory lesson to discuss the mechanics of the Upper Body Push-Up and follow-up with a demonstration of the exercise by yourself or by a skilled student.

2) Take time in the introductory lesson to individually assess the proper starting position for each student.

3) Emphasize the need to keep the legs and back straight throughout the entire performance of the exercise.

4) Make certain the hands are placed palms down beside the hips on the mat or on the floor with the fingers pointed forward.

5) As a variation for students with sufficient upper body and arm strength, have them hold the lifted body position for three to five seconds before slowly and carefully lowering the body to the mat or floor.

6) Mention the major muscle groups in the upper body and arms that are used to perform the Upper Body Push-Up.

7) Increase the number of repetitions as the students become stronger and show proficiency in performing the Upper Body Push-Up.

8) Instead of having the students perform a specific number of Upper Body Push-Ups, have them perform as many as possible within a designated period of time. Afterward, ask the students to honestly respond to the number they performed during the time period.

9) If Appropriate, encourage the students to follow-up by practicing/performing the Upper Body Push-Up away from the school setting. Make certain the students understand the need to practice/perform the Upper Body Push-Up in a safe and open space.

10) Ask the students in follow-up lessons whether or not they practiced/performed the Upper Body Push-Up away from the school setting. Commend the students who did their "homework" for being responsible and conscientious.

11) Assist students, if necessary.

PUSH-UP

STARTING POSITION
Assume a front leaning rest position on a mat or in an open space on the floor with the body being supported on semi-straightened arms positioned below the shoulders. Do not lock the arms to make them straight. The legs are together and straight with

the toes on the mat or floor. The hands are slightly greater than a shoulder-width apart with the fingers pointed forward. The eyes are focused on the mat or floor in front of the hands.

PERFORMANCE
Lower the body by bending the elbows until the chest or chin touches the mat or floor, then push the body upward by straightening the arms to return to the starting position. Throughout the performance of the Push-Up, the body is kept in a straight line from head to heels. Continue to perform the Push-Up a minimum of five times.

FINISHING POSITION
End in a front leaning rest position on a mat or in an open space on the floor with the body being supported on semi-straightened arms positioned below the shoulders. Do not lock the arms to make them straight. The legs are together and straight with the toes on the mat or floor. The hands are slightly greater than a shoulder-width apart with the fingers pointed forward. The eyes are focused on the mat or floor in front of the hands.

IMPORTANT TEACHING SUGGESTIONS

1) Take time in the introductory lesson to discuss the mechanics of the Push-Up and follow-up with a demonstration of the exercise by yourself or by a skilled student.

2) Take time in the introductory lesson to individually assess the proper starting position for each student and make necessary changes.

3) Emphasize the importance to keep the body straight throughout the entire exercise and to not allow the hips to drop to create a valley or to allow the hips to rise to create a mountain.

4) Make certain the hands are slightly greater than a shoulder-width apart with the fingers pointed forward.

5) Make certain the students lower their bodies to allow only the chest or chin to touch the mat or floor. The elbows should not be overly bent at the lowest point of the Push-Up.

6) Tell the students to allow a very slight bend in the arms at the highest point of the Push-Up. Discourage the students from locking their arms.

7) As a modification for students who are overweight, lack upper body and arm strength, or have a physical limitation in the lower extremities, allow these students to do Modified Push-Ups beginning on page 41. Be patient and supportive with these students and continually challenge them to give their very best effort and encourage them to perform to their maximum potential.

8) As a variation for students with sufficient upper body and arm strength, have them perform the Push-Up in a four count sequence: 1) halfway down, 2) reach lowest point, 3) halfway up, and 4) reach highest point.

9) As a variation for students with sufficient upper body and arm strength and confidence, have them perform the Push-Up by moving the hands a little closer together.

10) As a variation for students with sufficient upper body and arm strength and confidence, challenge them to push down with a lot of force to allow the body to rise quickly, then take the hands off the mat or floor to clap the hands together before returning the hands to their proper places on the mat or floor in the correct starting position.

11) Mention the major muscle groups in the upper body and arms that are used to perform the Push-Up.

12) Increase the number of repetitions as the students become stronger and show proficiency while performing the Push-Up.

13) Instead of having the students perform a specific number of Push-Ups, have them perform as many as possible within a designated period of time. Afterward, ask the students to honestly respond to the number they performed during the time period.

14) If appropriate, encourage the students to follow-up by practicing/performing the Push-Up away from the school setting. Make certain the students understand the need to practice/perform the Push-Up in a safe and open space.

15) Ask the students in follow-up lessons whether or not they practiced/performed the Push-Up away from the school setting. Commend the students who did their "homework" for being responsible and conscientious.

16) Assist students, if necessary.

MODIFIED PUSH-UP

STARTING POSITION
Assume a modified front leaning rest position on a mat or in an open space on the floor with the body from knees to head being supported on semi-straightened arms positioned below the shoulders. Do not lock the arms to make them straight. The legs and feet are together with the knees on the mat or floor. The feet are lifted diagonally backward. The hands are slightly greater than a shoulder-width apart with the fingers pointed forward. The eyes are focused on the mat or floor in front of the hands.

PERFORMANCE
Lower the body by bending the elbows until the chest or chin touches the mat or floor, then push the body upward by straightening the arms to return to the starting position. Throughout the performance of the Modified Push-Up, the body is kept in a straight line from head to knees. Continue to perform the Modified Push-Up a minimum of five times.

FINISHING POSITION
End in a modified front leaning rest position on a mat or in an open space on the floor with the body from knees to head being supported on a semi-straightened arms positioned below the shoulders. <u>Do not</u> lock the arms to make them straight. The legs and feet are together with the knees on the mat or floor. The feet are lifted diagonally backward. The hands are slightly greater than a shoulder-width apart with the fingers pointed forward. The eyes are focused on the mat or floor in front of the hands.

IMPORTANT TEACHING SUGGESTIONS

1) Take time in the introductory lesson to discuss the mechanics of the Modified Push-Up and follow-up with a demonstration of the exercise by yourself or by a skilled student.

2) Take time in the introductory lesson to individually assess the proper starting position for each student and make necessary changes.

3) Emphasize the need to keep the body straight from knees to head throughout the entire exercise and to not allow the hips to drop to create a valley or to allow the hips to rise to create a mountain.

4) Make certain the hands are slightly greater than a shoulder-width apart with the fingers pointed forward.

5) Make certain the students lower their bodies to allow only the chest or chin to touch the mat or floor. The elbows should not be overly bent at the lowest point of the Modified Push-Up.

6) Tell the students to allow a very slight bend in the arms at the highest point of the Modified Push-Up. Discourage the students from locking their arms.

7) The Modified Push-Up is an appropriate exercise to replace the Push-Up for students who are overweight, lack upper body and arm strength, or have a physical limitation in the lower extremities.

8) If possible, encourage students to attempt Push-Ups (see pages 39 and 40 for teaching guidelines) when they attain sufficient strength in the upper body and arms accompanied with self confidence. At first, have them try one Push-Up then perform Modified Push-Ups. If successful, increase the Push-Ups by one each time while lessening the number of Modified Push-Ups. Be patient and supportive with these students and continually challenge them to give their very best effort and encourage them to perform to their maximum potential.

9) As a variation for students with sufficient upper body and arm strength, have them perform the Modified Push-Up in a four count sequence: 1) halfway down, 2) reach lowest point, 3) halfway up, and 4) reach highest point.

10) Mention the major muscle groups in the upper body and arms that are used to perform the Modified Push-Up.

11) Increase the number of repetitions as the students become stronger and show proficiency while performing the Modified Push-Up.

12) Instead of having the students perform a specific number of Modified Push-Ups, have them perform as many as possible within a designated period of time.

Afterward, ask the students to honestly respond to the number they performed during the time period.

13) If appropriate, encourage the students to follow-up by practicing/performing the Modified Push-Up away from the school setting. Make certain the students understand the need to practice/perform the Modified Push-Up in a safe and open space.

14) Ask the students in follow-up lessons whether or not they practiced/performed the Modified Push-Up away from the school setting. Commend the students who did their "homework" for being responsible and conscientious.

15) Assist students, if necessary.

STATIC PUSH-UP

STARTING POSITION
Assume a front leaning rest position on a mat or in an open space on the floor with the body being supported on semi-straightened arms positioned below the shoulders. Do not lock the arms to make them straight. The legs are together and straight with the toes on the mat or floor. The hands are slightly greater than a shoulder-width apart with the fingers pointed forward. The eyes are focused on the mat or floor in front of the hands.

PERFORMANCE
Lower the body by bending the elbows until they are flexed at approximately 90° angles. Hold the position for three seconds. Then, push the body upward by straightening the arms to return to the starting position. Throughout the performance of the Static Push-Up, the body is kept in a straight line from head to heels. Continue to perform the Static Push-Up for a minimum of five times.

FINISHING POSITION
End in a front leaning rest position on a mat or in an open space on the floor with the body being supported on semi-straightened arms positioned below the shoulders. Do not lock the arms to make them straight. The legs are together and straight with the toes on the mat or floor. The hands are slightly greater than a shoulder-width apart with the fingers pointed forward. The eyes are focused on the mat or floor in front of the hands.

IMPORTANT TEACHING SUGGESTIONS

1) Take time in the introductory lesson to discuss the mechanics of the Static

Push-Up and follow-up with a demonstration of the exercise by yourself or by a skilled student.

2) Take time in the introductory lesson to individually assess the proper starting position for each student and make necessary changes.

3) Emphasize the need to keep the body straight throughout the entire exercise and to not allow the hips to drop to create a valley or to allow the hips to rise to create a mountain.

4) Make certain the hands are slightly greater than a shoulder-width apart with the fingers pointed forward.

5) Make certain the students lower their bodies to a level in which the elbows are flexed at approximately 90° angles.

6) Tell the students to allow a very slight bend in the arms at the highest point of the Static Push-Up. Discourage the students from locking their arms.

7) As a modification for students who are overweight, lack upper body and arm strength, or have a physical limitation in the lower extremities, allow these students to modify the Static Push-Up by performing the exercise on their knees instead of their toes. Be patient and supportive with these students and continually challenge them to give their very best effort and encourage them to perform to their maximum potential.

8) If possible, encourage students who are performing Modified Static Push-Ups to attempt Static Push-Ups when they attain sufficient strength in the upper body and arms accompanied with self confidence. At first, have them try one Static Push-Up then perform Modified Static Push-Ups. If successful, increase the Static Push-Ups by one each time while lessening the number of Modified Static Push-Ups. Be patient and supportive with these students and continually challenge them to give their very best effort and encourage them to perform to their maximum potential.

9) As a variation for students with sufficient upper body and arm strength and confidence, challenge them to hold the flexed arm position for a longer period of time. Begin with four seconds. If successful, increase the seconds by one each class period up to a maximum of ten seconds.

10) As a variation for students with sufficient upper body and arm strength and confidence, challenge them to hold the first flexed arm position for ten seconds. Decrease the time for the flexed arm position by one second each time the Static Push-Up is performed until the flexed arm position is held for only one second. Thus, ten Static Push-Ups are performed with varying flexed arm time held positions.

11) Mention the major muscle groups in the upper body and arms that are used to perform the Static Push-Up.

12) If appropriate, encourage the students to follow-up by practicing/performing the Static Push-Up away from the school setting. Make certain the students understand the need to practice/perform the Static Push-Up in a safe and open space.

13) Ask the students in follow-up lessons whether or not they practiced/performed the Static Push-Up away from the school setting. Commend the students who did their "homework" for being responsible and conscientious.

14) Assist students, if necessary.

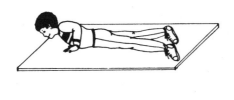

SIDE STANDER

STARTING POSITION

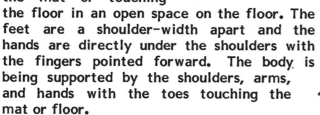

Assume a Modified Push-Up position with the chest touching the mat or touching the floor in an open space on the floor. The feet are a shoulder-width apart and the hands are directly under the shoulders with the fingers pointed forward. The body is being supported by the shoulders, arms, and hands with the toes touching the mat or floor.

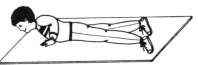

PERFORMANCE

Push down on the hands to lift the body while keeping the body straight. When the arms are fully extended, raise the right hand and right foot off the mat or floor. Rotate the body ¼ turn to the right so the right hand is extended upward directly above the left hand and the right foot is positioned above the left foot. Then, slowly return the right hand, right foot, and body to their original positions. Repeat the process by lifting and rotating the left side of the body ¼ turn to the left. Raise the left hand and left foot off the mat or floor to extend the left hand directly above the right hand and to position the left foot above the right foot. Then, slowly return the left hand, left foot, and body to their original positions. Continue to perform the Side Stander a minimum of five times.

FINISHING POSITION

End in a Modified Push-Up position with the chest touching the mat or touching the floor in an open space on the floor. The feet are a shoulder-width apart and the hands are directly under the shoulders with the fingers pointed forward. The body is being supported by the shoulders, arms, and hands with the toes touching the mat or floor.

IMPORTANT TEACHING SUGGESTIONS

1) Take time in the introductory lesson to discuss the mechanics of the Side Stander and follow-up with a demonstration of the exercise by yourself or by a skilled student.

2) Take time in the introductory lesson to individually assess the proper starting position for each student and make necessary changes.

3) Emphasize the need to keep the body straight throughout all phases of the exercise and to not allow the hips to drop to create a valley or to allow the hips to rise to create a mountain.

4) Discuss the differences between the Side Stander and a regulation Push-Up.

5) As a modification for students who are overweight or students who lack upper body and arm strength, have them perform the starting and finishing positions with the chest and body touching the mat or floor. Also, allow the hips to drop slightly when the body is lifted off the mat or floor. Lastly, have these students do less than a ¼ turn to lift the hand and corresponding foot off the mat or floor. Be patient and supportive with these students and continually challenge them to give their very best effort and encourage them to perform to their maximum potential.

6) As a modification for students who are overweight or students who lack upper body and arm strength, have them perform the exercise with their knees on the mat or floor instead of their toes. All phases of the exercise will be identical to the regulation Side Stander with the exception of the knee being raised off the mat or floor instead of the foot. For students who need further modification, have them perform the starting and finishing positions with their chest and body touching the mat or floor. Be patient and supportive with these students and continually challenge them to give their best effort and perform to their maximum potential.

7) Discuss the word "balance" and the need to "balance" the body above the support hand and foot when rotating the body in ¼ turns to the left or right.

8) For certain students who need to perform the Side Stander in a modified form, have them begin with regulation Side Standers and, when necessary, change to Modified Side Standers.

9) Discuss the need to have sufficient strength in the upper body and arms to perform the exercise correctly and safely. Also, discuss the need to have adequate strength within the midsection of the body to keep the body straight throughout the exercise.

10) Mention the major muscle groups in the body that are used to perform the Side Stander.

11) Instead of having the students perform a specific number of Side Standers, have them perform as many as possible within a designated period of time. Afterward, ask the students to honestly respond to the number they performed during the time period.

12) If appropriate, encourage the students to follow-up by practicing/performing the Side Stander away from the school setting. Make certain the students understand the need to practice/perform the Side Stander in a safe and open space.

13) Ask the students in follow-up lessons whether or not they practiced/performed the Side Stander away from the school setting. Commend the students who did their "homework" for being responsible and conscientious.

14) Assist students, if necessary.

PULL-UP

STARTING POSITION
Assume a straight arm and straight body hanging position with the hands grasping the bar with an overhand grip (palms facing forward). The hands are a shoulder-width apart. The toes are pointed downward with the feet a short distance above the mat or floor.

PERFORMANCE
Pull the body upward until the chin clears the top of the bar. Then, lower the body until the arms become fully extended. Throughout the process stabilize the body so there is no kicking, jerking, or swinging the body and/or legs. Continue to perform as many Pull-Ups as possible.

FINISHING POSITION
End in a straight arm and straight body hanging position with the hands grasping the bar with an overhand grip (palms facing forward). The hands are a shoulder-width apart. The toes are pointed downward with the feet a short distance above the mat or floor.

IMPORTANT TEACHING SUGGESTIONS

1) Take time in the introductory lesson to discuss the mechanics of the Pull-Up and follow-up with a demonstration of the exercise by yourself or by a skilled student.

2) Take time in the introductory lesson to individually assess the proper starting position for each student and make necessary changes.

3) Emphasize the importance of using the overhand grip (palms facing forward).

4) Stress the need to place and keep the hands a shoulder-width apart on the bar.

5) Make certain the students begin each Pull-Up with the arms fully extended.

6) Tell the students the chin must completely clear the top of the bar before the body can be lowered by fully extending the arms.

7)   Discuss the need to stabilize the body throughout the performance of the Pull-Up without kicking, jerking, or swinging the body and/or legs.

8)   Make certain the feet do not touch the mat or floor during the performance of the Pull-Up. The feet are a short distance above the mat or floor.

9)   Emphasize the importance of straightening the arms slowly to return the body to the fully extended arm and body hanging position.

10) As a modification for students who are overweight or lack upper body and arm strength, allow these students to do Modified Pull-Ups (see pages 48 and 49 for teaching guidelines). Be patient and supportive with these students and continually challenge them to give their very best effort and encourage them to perform to their maximum potential.

11) Challenge the students to perform as many Pull-Ups as possible.

12) Mention the major muscle groups in the upper body and arms that are used to perform the Pull-Up.

13) If appropriate, encourage the students to follow-up by practicing/performing the Pull-Up away from the school setting. Make certain the students understand the need to practice/perform the Pull-Up in a safe and appropriate place.

14) Ask the students in follow-up lessons whether or not they were able to practice/-perform the Pull-Up away from the school setting. Commend the students who were able to locate a safe and appropriate place.

15) Assist students, if necessary.

MODIFIED PULL-UP

STARTING POSITION
Assume a straight arm and straight body leaning backward position with the hands grasping the bar with an overhand grip (palms facing forward). The height of the bar is adjusted to a chest level standing position of the performer. The hands are a shoulder-width apart. The feet are positioned on a mat or floor directly beneath the bar. The body forms an angle of approximately 45° with the bar.

PERFORMANCE
Raise the body so the chest touches the bar then slowly lower the body to return to the starting position. Throughout the process the body is kept in a straight line. The chest touches the bar when the body is raised and the arms are straight when the body is lowered. Continue to perform as many Modified Pull-Ups as possible.

FINISHING POSITION
End in a straight arm and straight body leaning backward position with the hands grasping the bar with an overhand grip (palms facing forward). The hands are a shoulder-width apart. The feet are positioned on a mat or floor directly beneath the bar. The body is at approximately a 45° angle with the bar.

IMPORTANT TEACHING SUGGESTIONS

1) Take time in the introductory lesson to discuss the mechanics of the Modified Pull-Up and follow-up with a demonstration of the exercise by yourself or a skilled student.

2) Take time in the introductory lesson to individually assess the proper starting position for each student and make necessary changes.

3) Emphasize the importance of keeping the body straight throughout the entire exercise.

4) Make certain the feet are positioned on a mat or floor directly beneath the bar.

5) Explain the need to use the overhand grip since the use of the underhand grip would change the exercise to a Modified Chin-Up.

6) Stress the need to do a complete range of movement for each Modified Pull-Up by raising the body to touch the chest to the bar and lowering the body until the arms are straight.

7) The Modified Pull-Up is an appropriate exercise to replace the Pull-Up for students who are overweight or lack upper body and arm strength.

8) If possible, encourage students to attempt Pull-Ups (refer to page 47 for teaching guidelines) when they attain sufficient strength in the upper body and arms accompanied with self-confidence. At first, have them try one Pull-Up then perform Modified Pull-Ups. If successful, increase the Pull-Ups by one each time while lessening the number of Modified Pull-Ups. Be patient and supportive with these students and continually challenge them to give their very best effort and encourage them to perform to their maximum potential.

9) Mention the major muscle groups in the upper body and arms that are used to perform the Modified Pull-Up.

10) If appropriate, encourage the students to follow-up by practicing/performing the Modified Pull-Up away from the school setting. Make certain the students understand the need to practice/perform the Modified Pull-Up in a safe and appropriate place.

11) Ask the students in follow-up lessons whether or not they practiced/performed the Modified Pull-Up away from the school setting. Commend the students who were able to locate a safe and appropriate place.

12) Assist students, if necessary.

CHIN-UP

STARTING POSITION
Assume a straight arm and straight body hanging position with the hands grasping the bar with an underhand grip (palms facing backward). The hands are a shoulder-width apart. The toes are pointed downward with the feet a short distance above the mat or floor.

PERFORMANCE
Pull the body upward until the chin clears the top of the bar. Then, lower the body until the arms become fully extended. Throughout the process stabilize the body so there is no kicking, jerking, or swinging the body and/or legs. Continue to perform as many Chin-Ups as possible.

FINISHING POSITION
End in a straight arm and straight body hanging position with the hands grasping the bar with an underhand grip (palms facing backward). The hands are a shoulder-width apart. The toes are pointed downward with the feet a short distance above the mat or floor.

IMPORTANT TEACHING SUGGESTIONS

1) Take time in the introductory lesson to discuss the mechanics of the Chin-Up and follow-up with a demonstration of the exercise by yourself or by a skilled student.

2) Take time in the introductory lesson to individually assess the proper starting position for each student and make necessary changes.

3) Emphasize the importance of using the underhand grip (palms facing backward).

4) Stress the need to place and keep the hands a shoulders-width apart on the bar.

5) Make certain the students begin each Chin-Up with the arms fully extended.

6) Tell the students the chin must completely clear the top of the bar before the body can be lowered by fully extending the arms.

7) Discuss the need to stabilize the body throughout the performance of the Chin-Up without kicking, jerking, or swinging the body and/or legs.

8) Make certain the feet do not touch the mat or floor during the performance of the Chin-Up. The feet are a short distance above the mat or floor.

9) Emphasize the importance of straightening the arms slowly to return the body to the fully extended arm and body hanging position.

10) As a modification for students who are overweight or lack upper body and arm strength allow these students to do Modified Chin-Ups (refer to pages 51 and 52 for teaching guidelines). Be patient and supportive with these students and continually challenge them to give their very best effort and encourage them to perform to their maximum potential.

11) Challenge the students to perform as many Chin-Ups as possible.

12) Mention the major muscle groups in the upper body and arms that are used to perform the Chin-Up.

13) If appropriate, encourage the students to follow-up by practicing/performing the Chin-Up away from the school setting. Make certain the students understand the need to practice/perform the Chin-Up in a safe and appropriate place.

14) Ask the students in follow-up lessons whether or not they were able to practice/perform the Chin-Up away from the school setting. Commend the students who were able to locate a safe and appropriate place.

15) Assist students, if necessary.

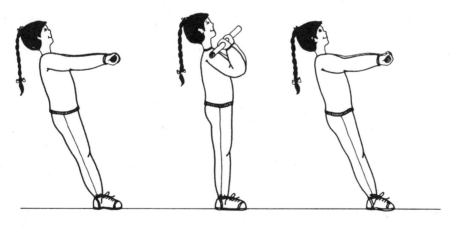

MODIFIED CHIN-UP

STARTING POSITION
Assume a straight arm and straight body leaning backward position with the hands grasping the bar with an underhand grip (palms facing backward). The height of the bar is adjusted to a chest level standing position of the performer. The hands are a shoulder-width apart. The feet are positioned on a mat or floor directly beneath the bar. The body forms an angle of approximately 45° with the bar.

PERFORMANCE
Raise the body so the chest touches the bar then slowly lower the body to return to the starting position. Throughout the process the body is kept in a straight line. The chest touches the bar when the body is raised and the arms are straight when the body is lowered. Continue to perform as many Modified Chin-Ups as possible.

FINISHING POSITION
End in a straight arm and straight body leaning backward position with the hands grasping the bar with an underhand grip (palms facing backward). The hands are a shoulder-width apart. The feet are positioned on a mat or floor directly beneath the bar. The body is at an angle of approximately 45° with the bar.

IMPORTANT TEACHING SUGGESTIONS

1) Take time in the introductory lesson to discuss the mechanics of the Modified Chin-Up and follow-up with a demonstration of the exercise by yourself or by a skilled student.

2) Take time in the introductory lesson to individually assess the proper starting position for each student and make necessary changes.

3) Emphasize the importance of keeping the body straight throughout the entire exercise.

4) Make certain the feet are positioned on a mat or floor directly beneath the bar.

5) Explain the need to use the underhand grip since the use of the overhand grip would change the exercise to a Modified Pull-Up.

6) Stress the need to do a complete range of movement for each Modified Chin-Up by raising the body to touch the chest to the bar and lowering the body until the arms are straight.

7) The Modified Chin-Up is an appropriate exercise to replace the Chin-Up for students who are overweight or lack upper body and arm strength.

8) If possible, encourage students to attempt Chin-Ups (refer to page 50 for teaching guidelines) when they attain sufficient strength in the upper body and arms accompanied with self confidence. At first have them try one Chin-Up then perform Modified Chin-Ups. If successful, increase the Chin-Ups by one each time while lessening the number of Modified Chin-Ups. Be patient and supportive with these students and continually challenge them to give their very best effort and encourage them to perform to their maximum potential.

9) Mention the major muscle groups in the upper body and arms that are used to perform the Modified Chin-Up.

10) If appropriate, encourage the students to follow-up by practicing/performing the Modified Chin-Up away from the school setting. Make certain the students understand the need to practice/perform the Modified Chin-Up in a safe and appropriate place.

11) Ask the students in follow-up lessons whether or not they practiced/performed the Modified Chin-Up away from the school setting. Commend the students who were able to locate a safe and appropriate place.

12) Assist students, if necessary.

BENT ARM HANG

STARTING POSITION
Assume a standing position on a mat or floor facing a bar that is slightly higher than one's height. Grasp the bar with an overhand grip (palms facing forward). Hands are a shoulder-width apart.

PERFORMANCE
Attain a raised body position with the chin above the bar and the feet off the mat or floor. The elbows are flexed and the chest is close to the bar. The body is stabilized and the legs are straight with the toes pointed downward. Hold the Bent Arm Hang position for as long as possible. Upon completion, return the feet to the mat or floor by slowly straightening the arms. Be certain the head tilts back slightly to free the chin from the over-the-bar position.

FINISHING POSITION
End in a standing position on a mat or floor with the hands in an overhand grip (palms facing forward) on the bar. The hands are a shoulder-width apart.

IMPORTANT TEACHING SUGGESTIONS

1) Take time in the introductory lesson to discuss the mechanics of the Bent Arm Hang and follow-up with a demonstration of the exercise by yourself or by a skilled student.

2) Take time in the introductory lesson to individually assess the proper starting position for each student and make necessary changes.

3) Emphasize the importance of using the overhand grip (palms facing forward).

4) Stress the need to place and keep the hands a shoulder-width apart on the bar.

5) Challenge each student to pull his/her body upward to attain the proper Bent Arm Hang position instead of jumping upward to attain the position.

6) Tell the students to keep the chin above the bar without touching the bar.

7) Discuss the need to stabilize the body in the proper Bent Arm Hang position without kicking, jerking, or swinging the body and/or legs.

8) Make certain the students keep their chests close to the bar in the proper Bent Arm Hang position.

9) Challenge the students to hold the Bent Arm Hang position as long as possible. When the proper Bent Arm Hang position is attained, begin to time the student. Timing should stop when the chin touches or drops below the bar.

10) Make certain the students understand the importance of straightening the arms slowly while tilting the head slightly backward to return the feet to the mat or floor.

11) As a modification for students who are overweight or lack upper body arm strength, lower the bar to a point that permits the students' toes to barely touch the mat or floor while being in the proper Bent Arm Hang position. Be patient and supportive with these students and continually challenge them to give their very best effort and encourage them to perform to their maximum potential.

12) As a variation have the students use the underhand grip (palms facing backward) to perform the Bent Arm Hang.

13) Mention the major muscle groups in the upper body and arms that are used to perform the Bent Arm Hang.

14) If appropriate, encourage the students to follow-up by practicing/performing the Bent Arm Hang away from the school setting. Make certain the students understand the need to practice/perform the Bent Arm Hang in a safe and appropriate place.

15) Ask the students in follow-up lessons whether or not they were able to practice/-perform the Bent Arm Hang away from the school setting. Commend the students who were able to locate a safe and appropriate place.

16) Assist students, if necessary.

BACK FLATTENER

STARTING POSITION
Assume a lying down supine position with the knees bent at a 90° angle on the mat or in an open space on the floor. The arms are fully extended and resting at the sides of the body with the hands palms down on the mat or floor. The feet are together with the feet flat on the mat or floor.

PERFORMANCE
Contract the abdominal muscles to press the lower back to the mat or floor and hold for three to five seconds. Then, relax the abdominal muscles to return to the starting position. Continue to perform the Back Flattener a minimum of ten times.

FINISHING POSITION
End in a lying down supine position with the knees bent at a 90° angle on the mat or in an open space on the floor. The arms are fully extended and resting at the sides of the body with the hands palms down on the mat or floor. The feet are together with the feet flat on the mat or floor.

IMPORTANT TEACHING SUGGESTIONS

1) Take time in the introductory lesson to discuss the mechanics of the Back Flattener and follow-up with a demonstration of the exercise by yourself or by a skilled student.

2) Take time in the introductory lesson to individually assess the proper starting position for each student.

3) Make certain the students keep their knees bent at a 90° angle and keep their feet flat on the mat or floor throughout the entire exercise.

4) Use the teaching cue "touch the lower back to the mat or floor" to reinforce the need to press the lower back to the mat or floor.

5) Discuss how the abdominal muscles help in the performance of certain parallel bar stunts such as Skin The Cat and Swing.

6) Increase the time the abdominal muscles contract to press the lower back to the mat or floor to a maximum of ten seconds as the students become stronger and show proficiency while performing the Back Flattener.

7) If appropriate, encourage the students to follow-up by practicing/performing the Back Flattener away from the school setting. Make certain the students understand the need to practice/perform the Back Flattener in a safe and open space.

8) Ask the students in follow-up lessons whether or not they practiced/performed the Back Flattener away from the school setting. Commend the students who did their "homework" for being responsible and conscientious.

9) Assist students, if necessary.

ABDOMINAL CURL-UP

STARTING POSITION
Assume a lying down supine position with the knees bent at a 90° angle on the mat or in an open space on the floor. The feet are slightly apart and flat on the mat or floor. The arms are across the chest with the hands placed on opposite shoulders.

PERFORMANCE
Slowly curl the head, shoulders, and upper body off the mat or floor. In the process, the feet remain in contact with the mat or floor and the lower back touches the mat or floor. Hold the Curl-Up position for three seconds. Then, slowly lower the upper body, shoulders, and head to return to their original positions. Continue to perform the Abdominal Curl-Up a minimum of twenty times.

FINISHING POSITION
End in a lying down supine position with the knees bent at a 90° angle on the mat or in an open space on the floor. The feet are slightly apart and flat on the mat or floor. The arms are across the chest with the hands placed on opposite shoulders.

IMPORTANT TEACHING SUGGESTIONS

1) Take time in the introductory lesson to discuss the mechanics of the Abdominal Curl-Up and follow-up with a demonstration of the exercise by yourself or by a skilled student.

2) Take time in the introductory lesson to individually assess the proper starting position for each student.

3) Make certain the students keep their knees bent at a 90° angle and keep their feet flat on the mat or floor throughout the entire exercise.

4) Stress the need to keep the arms crossed with the hands placed on opposite shoulders.

5) Discuss the term "curl" and relate it to the "curl-up" progression of the head, shoulders, and upper back moving upward and downward.

6) Tell the students to have the lower back touch the mat or floor during each part of the Curl-Up progression.

7) Discuss how the abdominal muscles help in the performance of certain parallel bar stunts such as Skin The Cat and Swing.

8) Increase the time of the Curl-Up position to a maximum of ten seconds as the students become stronger and show proficiency while performing the Abdominal Curl-Up.

9) If appropriate, encourage the students to follow-up by practicing/performing the Abdominal Curl-Up away from the school setting. Make certain the students understand the need to practice/perform the Abdominal Curl-Up in a safe and open space.

10) Ask the students in follow-up lessons whether or not they practiced/performed the Abdominal Curl-Up away from the school setting. Commend the students who did their "homework" for being responsible and conscientious.

11) Assist students, if necessary.

BENT KNEE SIT-UP

STARTING POSITION
Assume a lying down supine position with the knees bent at a 90° angle on the mat or in an open space on the floor. The feet are slightly apart and flat on the mat or floor. Place the hands palms down on the thighs. Lift the head and shoulders off the mat or floor.

PERFORMANCE
Slowly curl the upper body off the mat or floor while sliding the hands forward until the wrists touch the knees. Then, slowly curl the upper body downward while sliding the hands backward to return the hands to their original positions. In the process, the arms are straight, the feet remain in contact with the mat or floor, and the lower back touches the mat or floor. Continue to perform the Bent Knee Sit-Up a minimum of twenty times.

FINISHING POSITION
End in a lying down supine position with the knees bent at a 90° angle on the mat or in an open space on the floor. The feet are slightly apart and flat on the mat or floor. The hands are palms down on the thighs and the head and shoulders are lifted off the mat or floor.

IMPORTANT TEACHING SUGGESTIONS

1) Take time in the introductory lesson to discuss the mechanics of the Bent Knee Sit-Up and follow-up with a demonstration of the exercise by yourself or by a skilled student.

2) Take time in the introductory lesson to individually assess the proper starting position for each student.

3) Make certain the students keep their knees bent at a 90° angle and keep their feet flat on the mat or floor throughout the entire exercise.

4) Stress the need to keep the arms straight while sliding the hands over the thighs until the wrists touch the knees during the first part of the exercise. Also, stress the need to keep the arms straight while sliding the hands over the thighs to return the hands to their original positions during the second part of the exercise.

5) Discuss the term "curl" and relate it to the "curl-up" movement of the upper body moving upward and downward.

6) Tell the students to have the lower back touch the mat or floor during each part of the curl-up progression.

7) Discuss how the abdominal muscles help in the performance of certain parallel bar stunts such as Skin The Cat and Swing.

8) Increase the number of Bent Knee Sit-Ups as the students become stronger and show proficiency while performing the Bent Knee Sit-Up.

9) Instead of having the students perform a specific number of Bent Knee Sit-Ups, have them perform as many as possible within a designated period of time. Afterward, ask the students to honestly respond to the number they performed during the time period.

10) As a modification for students who lack the abdominal strength to slide the wrists to the knees, challenge these students to slide the hands as far as possible toward the knees; however, make certain these students keep their heads and shoulders off the mat or floor during the performance of the modified Bent Knee Sit-Up.

11) If appropriate, encourage the students to follow-up by practicing/performing the Bent Knee Sit-Up away from the school setting. Make certain the students understand the need to practice/perform the Bent Knee Sit-Up in a safe and open space.

12) Ask the students in follow-up lessons whether or not they practiced/performed the Bent Knee Sit-Up away from the school setting. Commend the students who did their "homework" for being responsible and conscientious.

13) Assist students, if necessary.

Chapter – 4

MOUNTS

INTRODUCTION

The Mounts Chapter includes a detailed explanation of nine parallel bars mounts. Each explanation includes three phrases: Starting Position, Performance, and Finishing Position. In addition, each parallel bars mount has a list of Important Teaching Suggestions and a Spotting Hints section.

STRAIGHT ARM SUPPORT AT END MOUNT

STARTING POSITION
Begin in a bent leg standing position at the end of the parallel bars with the heels off the mat so the weight is balanced above the balls of the feet. The arms are straight with the shoulders positioned directly in front of the bars and the hands are in overhand grip positions on the ends of the bars. The head is level with the eyes focused forward.

PERFORMANCE
While maintaining a firm grip, jump forward and upward while pushing down on the bars to assume a balanced Straight Arm Support position above and between the ends of the bars.

FINISHING POSITION
End in a Straight Arm Support At End Mount position at the end of the parallel bars. The arms are straight and positioned along the sides of the body. The head is level and the body is straight up and down with the shoulders positioned directly above the hands. The toes are pointed downward.

IMPORTANT TEACHING SUGGESTIONS

1) Take time in the introductory lesson to discuss the mechanics of the Straight Arm Support At End Mount and follow-up with a demonstration of the mount by yourself or by a skilled student. If possible, reinforce the discussion and demonstration with a Straight Arm Support At End Mount chart and/or a related audiovisual aid.

2) Take time in the introductory lesson to individually assess the proper execution of the mount and make necessary corrections, if needed.

3) Teach the Straight Arm Support (refer to page 78 for teaching guidelines) as the lead-up stunt to the Straight Arm Support At End Mount.

4) Emphasize the need to perform the mount above a well matted area.

5) Stress the importance of using the overhand grip.

6) Make certain the students understand the importance of using a firm grip throughout the performance of the mount.

7) Stress the need to jump forward and upward to assume the proper Straight Arm Support position above and between the ends of the bars.

8) After jumping, tell the students to push downward on the bars with force to help attain the proper Straight Arm Support position above and between the ends of the bars.

9) Stress the need to stop in a balanced Straight Arm Support position directly above and between the hands. The movements must be controlled so that balance is not lost resulting in the student falling forward or backward.

10) Discuss the term "balance" and the role it plays after the performance when the body is in a Straight Arm Support position.

11) Encourage smooth movements with minimum swinging of the body during the performance of the mount.

12) Assist students, if necessary.

SPOTTING HINTS

Position yourself next to the end of the parallel bars while being directly beside the student's closest hand. Grasp the student's near wrist with your front hand and grasp the back of the student's closest upper arm near the arm pit with your back hand. The fingers of your back hand circle toward the front of the student's upper arm. On your signal, instruct the student to perform the Straight Arm Support At End Mount. Give the student the necessary forward lift with your back hand to assume the proper or a modified Straight Arm Support At End Mount position at the end of the parallel bars. If the student achieves the proper Straight Arm Support At End Mount position, loosen your grip(s) without losing physical contact in order to give the student some independence while performing the mount; however, be ready to tighten your grip(s) if the student is unable to balance and/or support his/her body in the proper Straight Arm Support At End Mount position. Make certain you position yourself properly so as not to place undue pressure on your lower back or other potentially weak areas of your body. Do not overspot. Instead, have the student perform the Straight Arm Support At End Mount by providing a minimum amount of spotting necessary to allow for a successful and safe performance of the mount. Continue to give individualized assistance using the preceding method. If possible, encourage the student to practice the Straight Arm Support At End Mount without assistance.

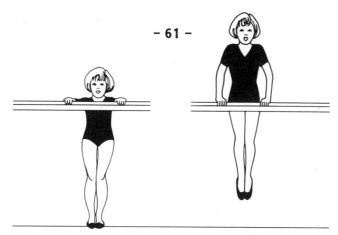

STRAIGHT ARM SUPPORT AT SIDE MOUNT

STARTING POSITION
Begin in a bent leg standing position at the side of the parallel bars with the heels off the mat so the weight is balanced above the balls of the feet. The arms are straight with the shoulders positioned directly in front of the near bar and the hands are in overhand grip positions on the bar. The head is level with the eyes focused forward.

PERFORMANCE
While maintaining a firm grip, jump forward and upward while pushing down on the bar to assume a balanced Straight Arm Support position against the side of the bar.

FINISHING POSITION
End in a Straight Arm Support At Side Mount position against the bar. The arms are straight and positioned along the sides of the body. The head is level and the body is straight up and down with the shoulders positioned directly above the hands. The hips are pressed against the bar and the toes are pointed downward.

IMPORTANT TEACHING SUGGESTIONS

1) Take time in the introductory lesson to discuss the mechanics of the Straight Arm Support At Side Mount and follow-up with a demonstration of the mount by yourself or by a skilled student. If possible, reinforce the discussion and demonstration with a Straight Arm Support At Side Mount chart and/or a related audiovisual aid.

2) Take time in the introductory lesson to individually assess the proper execution of the mount and make necessary corrections, if needed.

3) Teach the Straight Arm Support (refer to page 78 for teaching guidelines) as the lead-up stunt to the Straight Arm Support At Side Mount.

4) Emphasize the need to perform the mount above a well matted area.

5) Stress the importance of using the overhand grip.

6) Make certain the students understand the importance of using a firm grip throughout the performance of the mount.

7) Stress the need to jump forward and upward to assume the proper Straight Arm Support position above and against the bar.

8) After jumping, tell the students to push downward on the bar with force to help attain the proper Straight Arm Support position above and against the bar.

9) Stress the need to stop in a balanced Straight Arm Support position directly above and against the bar. The movements must be controlled so that balance is not lost resulting in the student falling forward or backward.

10) Discuss the term "balance" and the role it plays after the performance when the body is against the bar in a Straight Arm Support position.

11) Tell the students who lack sufficient upper body strength to be able to perform the Straight Arm Support At Side Mount position against the bar to compensate by bending slightly at the waist to place the upper body above and slightly in front of the bar. By modifying the Straight Arm Support At Side Mount, the students will be able to hold the position without having to lower the feet to the mat.

12) Assist students, if necessary.

SPOTTING HINTS

Position yourself beside the parallel bars and facing the student. Grasp the student's near wrist with your inside hand and grasp the back of the student's closest upper arm near the arm pit with your outside hand. The fingers of your outside hand circle toward the front of the student's upper arm. On your signal, instruct the student to perform the Straight Arm Support At Side Mount. Give the student the necessary forward lift with your outside hand to assume the proper Straight Arm Support At End Mount position against the bar. If the student achieves the proper Straight Arm Support At Side Mount position, loosen your grip(s) without losing physical contact in order to give the student some independence while performing the mount; however, be ready to tighten your grip(s) if the student is unable to balance and/or support his/her body in the proper Straight Arm Support At Side Mount position against the bar. Make certain you position yourself properly so as not to place undue pressure on your lower back or other potentially weak areas of your body. <u>Do not</u> overspot. Instead, have the student perform the Straight Arm Support At Side Mount by providing a minimum amount of spotting necessary to allow for a successful and safe performance of the mount. Continue to give individualized assistance using the preceding method. If possible, encourage the student to practice the Straight Arm Support At Side Mount without assistance.

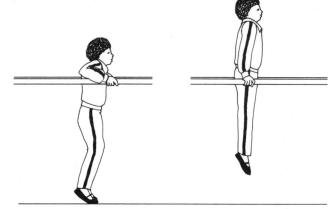

STRAIGHT ARM SUPPORT IN THE MIDDLE MOUNT

STARTING POSITION
Begin in a bent leg standing position in the middle of the parallel bars with the heels off the mat so the weight is balanced above the balls of the feet. The arms are bent with the insides of the upper arms resting on or positioned above the bars. The shoulders are located between the elbows and wrists and directly above the balls of the feet. The hands are in overhand grip positions on the bars and the head is level with the eyes focused forward.

PERFORMANCE
While maintaining a firm grip, jump upward while pushing down on the bars to assume a balanced Straight Arm Support position above and between the bars.

FINISHING POSITION
End in a Straight Arm Support position in the middle of the parallel bars. The arms are straight and positioned along the sides of the body. The head is level and the body is straight up and down with the shoulders positioned directly above the hands. The toes are pointed downward.

IMPORTANT TEACHING SUGGESTIONS

1) Take time in the introductory lesson to discuss the mechanics of the Straight Arm Support In The Middle Mount and follow-up with a demonstration of the mount by yourself or by a skilled student. If possible, reinforce the discussion and demonstration with a Straight Arm Support In The Middle Mount chart and/or a related audiovisual aid.

2) Take time in the introductory lesson to individually assess the proper execution of the mount and make necessary corrections, if needed.

3) Teach the Straight Arm Support (refer to page 000 for teaching guidelines) as the lead-up stunt to the Straight Arm Support In The Middle Mount.

4) Emphasize the need to perform the mount above a well matted area.

5) Stress the importance of using the overhand grip.

6) Make certain the students understand the importance of using a firm grip throughout the performance of the mount.

7) Discuss the need to jump directly upward to assume the proper Straight Arm Support position above and between the middle of the bars.

8) After jumping, tell the students to push downward on the bars with force to help attain the proper Straight Arm Support position above and between the middle of the bars.

9) Stress the importance of keeping the shoulders directly above the hands throughout the performance of the mount while keeping the head level and the body in a straight up and down position.

10) Encourage smooth movements with minimum swinging of the body during the performance of the mount.

11) Assist students, if necessary.

SPOTTING HINTS

Position yourself next to the middle of the parallel bars while being directly beside the student's closest hand. Grasp the student's near wrist with your front hand and grasp the back of the student's closest upper arm near the arm pit with your back hand. The fingers of your back hand circle toward the front of the upper arm. On your signal, instruct the student to perform the Straight Arm Support In The Middle Mount. Give the student the necessary lift with your back hand to assume the proper or a modified Straight Arm Support position above and between the middle of the bars. If the student achieves the proper Straight Arm Support position, loosen your grips without losing physical contact in order to give the student some independence while performing the mount; however, be ready to tighten your grips if the student is unable to balance and/or support his/her body in the proper Straight Arm Support position. Make certain you position yourself properly so as not to place undue pressure on your lower back or other potentially weak areas of your body. Do not overspot. Instead, have the student perform the Straight Arm Support In The Middle Mount by providing a minimum amount of spotting necessary to allow for a successful and safe performance of the mount. Continue to give individualized assistance using the preceding method. If possible, encourage the student to practice the Straight Arm Support In The Middle Mount without assistance.

STRADDLE SEAT AT END MOUNT

STARTING POSITION
Begin in a bent leg standing position at the end of the parallel bars with the heels off the mat so the weight is balanced above the balls of the feet. The arms are straight with the shoulders positioned directly in front of the bars and the hands are in overhand grip positions on the ends of the bars. The head is level with the eyes focused forward.

PERFORMANCE
While maintaining a firm grip, jump forward and upward while pushing down on the bars to assume a balanced Straight Arm Support position above and between the ends of the bars. Immediately, swing the legs forward and upward between the bars. As the legs pass slightly above the bars, separate them and place one leg across each bar to attain a Straddle Seat position.

FINISHING POSITION
End in a Straddle Seat At End Mount position at the end of the parallel bars with the legs straight and the toes pointed diagonally sideward. The back is straight and the head is level with the eyes focused forward. The hands are gripping the bars beside the buttocks.

IMPORTANT TEACHING SUGGESTIONS

1) Take time in the introductory lesson to discuss the mechanics of the Straddle Seat At End Mount and follow-up with a demonstration of the mount by yourself or by a skilled student. If possible, reinforce the discussion and demonstration with a Straddle Seat At End Mount chart and/or a related audiovisual aid.

2) Take time in the introductory lesson to individually assess the proper execution of the mount and make necessary corrections, if needed.

3) Teach the Straight Arm Support (refer to page 78 for teaching guidelines) and the Straddle Seat (refer to page 83 for teaching guidelines) as lead-up stunts to the Straddle Seat At End Mount.

4) Emphasize the need to perform the mount over a well matted area.

5) Stress the importance of using the overhand grip.

6) Make certain the students understand the importance of using a firm grip throughout the performance of the mount.

7) Stress the need to jump forward and upward to assume the proper momentary Straight Arm Support position above and between the ends of the bars.

8) After jumping, tell the students to push downward on the bars with force to help attain the proper momentary Straight Arm Support position above and between the ends of the bars.

9) Tell the students to swing the legs forward and upward after passing through the proper Straight Arm Support position.

10) Emphasize the need to swing the legs high enough to pass above the bars.

11) Instruct the students to separate the legs quickly when the legs are slightly above the bars.

12) Discuss the "polished" look of the Straddle Seat At End Mount by having the legs straight with the toes pointed diagonally sideward. Also, the back is straight and the head is level with the eyes focused forward. Lastly, the hands are griping the bars beside the buttocks.

13) Assist students, if necessary.

SPOTTING HINTS

Position yourself next to the end of the parallel bars while being directly beside the student's closest hand. Grasp the student's near wrist with your front hand and grasp the back of the student's closest upper arm near the arm pit with your back hand. The fingers of your back hand circle toward the front of the student's upper arm. On your signal, instruct the student to perform the Straddle Seat At End Mount. Give the student the necessary forward lift with your back hand to assume the proper momentary Straight Arm Support position at the end of the parallel bars. Continue to give the student the necessary support with your back hand to be able to maintain balance and stability while swinging the legs forward and upward to place them on the bars. Once the legs are on the bars, give verbal cues to remind the student about straight legs, pointed toes, straight back, head level with the eyes focused forward and proper hand positions on the bars. If possible, loosen your grips without losing physical contact in order to give the student some independence while performing the mount; however, be ready to tighten your grips if the student loses balance or stability and begins to fall forward or backward.

If the student can perform the first part of the mount and is able to assume the proper momentary Straight Arm Support position but has difficulty swinging the legs forward and upward to pass slightly above the bars, consider the following spotting modification. Maintain a strong, firm grip with your back hand on the student's upper arm, but release your grip on the student's wrist. Use your front hand to lift and guide the student's closest leg to help place it on top of the near bar. Most of the time, the student is able to place the far leg on the far bar at the same time or a little behind the placement of the near leg on the near bar. Make certain you give the necessary lift and support with your back hand on the student's upper arm to keep the student in the proper balanced upright position.

Make certain you position yourself properly in both spotting techniques so as not to place undue pressure on your lower back or other potentially weak areas of your body. Do not overspot. Instead, have the student perform the Straddle Seat At End Mount by providing a minimum amount of spotting necessary to allow for a successful and safe performance of the mount. Continue to give individualized assistance using the preceding methods. If possible, encourage the student to practice the Straddle Seat At End Mount without assistance.

STRADDLE SEAT IN THE MIDDLE MOUNT

STARTING POSITION
Begin in a bent leg standing position in the middle of the parallel bars with the heels off the mat so the weight is balanced above the balls of the feet. The arms are bent with the insides of the upper arms resting on or positioned above the bars. The shoulders are located between the elbows and wrists and directly above the balls of the feet. The hands are in overhand grip positions on the bars and the head is level with the eyes focused forward.

PERFORMANCE
While maintaining a firm grip, jump upward while pushing down on the bars to assume a balanced Straight Arm Support position above and between the middle of the parallel bars. Immediately, swing the legs forward and upward between the bars. As the legs swing slightly above the bars, separate and place one leg across each bar to attain a Straddle Seat position.

FINISHING POSITION

End in a Straddle Seat In The Middle Mount position in the middle of the parallel bars with the toes pointed diagonally sideward. The back is straight and the head is level with the eyes focused forward. The hands are gripping the bars beside the buttocks.

IMPORTANT TEACHING SUGGESTIONS

1) Take time in the introductory lesson to discuss the mechanics of the Straddle Seat In The Middle Mount and follow-up with a demonstration of the mount by yourself or by a skilled student. If possible, reinforce the discussion and demonstration with a Straddle Seat In The Middle Mount chart and/or a related audiovisual aid.

2) Take time in the introductory lesson to individually assess the proper execution of the mount and make necessary corrections, if needed.

3) Teach the Straight Arm Support (refer to page 78 for teaching guidelines) and to the Straddle Seat (refer to page 83 for teaching guidelines) as lead-up stunts to the Straddle Seat In The Middle Mount. .

4) Emphasize the need to perform the mount over a well matted area.

5) Stress the importance of using the overhand grip.

6) Make certain the students understand the importance of using a firm grip throughout the performance of the mount.

7) Stress the need to jump directly upward to assume the proper momentary Straight Arm Support position above and between the middle of the bars.

8) After jumping, tell the students to push downward on the bars with force to help attain the proper momentary Straight Arm Support position above and between the middle of the bars.

9) Tell the students to swing the legs forward and upward after passing through the proper Straight Arm Support position.

10) Emphasize the need to swing the legs high enough to pass above the bars.

11) Instruct the students to separate the legs quickly when the legs are slightly above the bars.

12) Discuss the "polished" look of the Straddle Seat In The Middle Mount by having the legs straight with the toes pointed diagonally sideward. Also, the back is straight and the head is level with the eyes focused forward.

13) Assist students, if necessary.

SPOTTING HINTS

Position yourself next to the parallel bars while being directly beside the student's closest hand. Grasp the student's near wrist with the front hand and grasp the back of the student's closest upper arm near the arm pit with your back hand. The fingers of your back hand circle toward the front of the student's upper arm. On your signal, instruct the student to perform the Straddle Seat In The Middle Mount. Give the student the necessary lift with your back hand to assume the proper momentary Straight Arm Support position in the middle of the parallel bars. Continue to give the student the necessary support with your back hand to be able to maintain balance and stability while swinging the legs forward and upward to place them on the bars. Once the legs are on the bars, give verbal cues to remind the student about straight legs, pointed toes, straight back, head level with the eyes focused forward, and proper hand positions on the bars. If possible, loosen your grips without losing physical contact in order to give the student some independence while performing the mount; however, be ready to tighten your grips if the student looses balance or stability and begins to fall forward or backward.

If the student can perform the first part of the mount and is able to assume the proper momentary Straight Arm Support position but has difficulty swinging the legs forward and upward to pass slightly above the bars, consider the following spotting modifications. Maintain a strong, firm grip with your back hand on the student's upper arm, but release your grip on the student's wrist. Use your front hand to lift and guide the student's closest leg to help the student place it on top of the near bar. Most of the time, the student is able to place the far leg on the far bar at the same time or a little behind the placement of the near leg on the near bar. Make certain you give the necessary lift and support with your back hand on the student's upper arm to keep the student in the proper balanced upright position.

Make certain you position yourself properly in both spotting techniques so as not to place undue pressure on your lower back or other potentially weak areas of your body. <u>Do not</u> overspot. Instead, have the student perform the Straddle Seat In The Middle Mount by providing a minimum amount of spotting necessary to allow for a successful and safe performance of the mount. Continue to give individualized assistance using the preceding methods. If possible, encourage the student to practice the Straddle Seat In The Middle Mount without assistance.

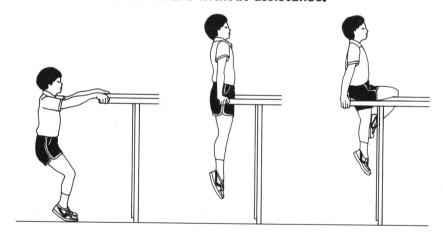

LEFT SIDE SEAT AT END MOUNT

STARTING POSITION
Begin in a bent leg standing position at the end of the parallel bars with the heels off the mat so the weight is balanced above the balls of the feet. The arms are straight with the shoulders positioned directly in front of the bars and the hands are in overhand grip positions on the ends of the bars. The head is level with the eyes focused forward.

PERFORMANCE

While maintaining a firm grip, jump forward and upward while pushing down on the bars to assume a balance Straight Arm Support position above and between the ends of the bars. Immediately, swing the legs forward and upward between the bars. As the legs swing slightly above the bars, swing them sideward over the left bar into a Left Side Seat position.

FINISHING POSITION

End in a Left Side Seat At End Mount position on the left bar. The left leg is vertically straight with the toes pointed downward. The right leg is bent with the upper leg from hip to knee sitting on the bar. The lower leg from knee to foot is angled toward the left knee with the right foot on top of the left knee. The back is straight and the head is level with the eyes focused forward. The left hand is gripping the bar behind the left buttocks and the right hand is gripping the other bar directly across from the right side of the body.

IMPORTANT TEACHING SUGGESTIONS

1) Take time in the introductory lesson to discuss the mechanics of the Left Side Seat At End Mount and follow-up with a demonstration of the mount by yourself or by a skilled student. If possible, reinforce the discussion and demonstration with a Left Side Seat At End Mount chart and/or a related audiovisual aid.

2) Take time in the introductory lesson to individually assess the proper execution of the mount and make necessary corrections, if needed.

3) Teach the Straight Arm Support (refer to page 78 for teaching guidelines) and the Left Side Seat (refer to page 84 for teaching guidelines) as lead-up stunts to the Left Side Seat At End Mount.

4) Emphasize the need to perform the mount over a well matted area.

5) Stress the importance of using the overhand grip.

6) Make certain the students understand the importance of using a firm grip throughout the performance of the mount.

7) Stress the need to jump forward and upward to assume the proper momentary Straight Arm Support position above and between the ends of the bars.

8) After jumping, tell the students to push downward on the bars with force to help attain the proper momentary Straight Arm Support position above and between the ends of the bars.

9) Tell the students to swing the legs forward and upward after passing through the proper Straight Arm Support position.

10) Emphasize the need to swing the legs high enough to pass above the bars.

11) Instruct the students to swing the legs over the left bar when the legs are slightly above the bars.

12) Discuss the "polished" look of the Left Side Seat by having the left leg vertically straight with the toes pointed downward, right foot on the left knee, back straight, head level with the eyes focused forward, and the hands gripping the bars in their proper positions.

13)   Assist students, if needed.

SPOTTING HINTS

Position yourself next to the end of the parallel bars while being directly beside the student's closest hand. Be on the side where the Left Side Seat At End Mount will be performed. Grasp the student's near wrist with your front hand and grasp the back of the student's closest upper arm near the arm pit with your back hand. The fingers of your back hand circle toward the front of the students upper arm. On your signal, instruct the student to perform the Left Side Seat At End Mount. Give the student the necessary forward lift with your back hand to assume the proper momentary Straight Arm Support Position at the end of the parallel bars. Continue to give the student the necessary support with your back hand to be able to maintain balance and stability while swinging the legs forward and upward to swing them sideward over the left bar. Once the student has attained the Left Side Seat position, give verbal cues to remind the student about the left leg being vertically straight with the toes pointed downward, right foot on the left knee, straight back, head level with the eyes focused forward, and proper hand positions on the bars. If possible, loosen the grips without losing physical contact in order to give the student some independence while performing the mount; however, be ready to tighten your grips if the student looses balance or begins to fall backward or sideward.

If the student can perform the first part of the mount and is able to assume the proper momentary Straight Arm Support position but has difficulty swinging the legs forward, upward, and over the bar, consider the following spotting modification. Maintain a strong, firm grip with your back hand on the student's upper arm, but release the grip on the student's wrist. Use the front hand to lift and guide the student's legs to help the student swing them over the left bar. Make certain you give the necessary lift and support with your back hand on the student's upper arm to keep the student in the proper balanced upright position.

Make certain you position yourself properly in both spotting techniques so as not to place undue pressure on your lower back or other potentially weak areas of the body. Do not overspot. Instead, have the student perform the Left Side Seat At End Mount by providing a minimum amount of spotting necessary to allow for a successful and safe performance of the mount. Continue to give individualized assistance using the preceding methods. If possible, encourage the student to practice the Left Side Seat At End Mount without assistance.

RIGHT SIDE SEAT AT END MOUNT

STARTING POSITION
Begin in a bent leg standing position at the end of the parallel bars with the heels off the mat so the weight is balanced above the balls of the feet. The arms are straight with the shoulders positioned directly in front of the bars and the hands are in overhand grip positions on the ends of the bars. The head is level with the eyes focused forward.

PERFORMANCE
While maintaining a firm grip, jump forward and upward while pushing down on the bars to assume a balanced Straight Arm Support position above and between the ends of the bars. Immediately, swing the legs forward and upward between the bars. As the legs swing slightly above the bars, swing them sideward over the right bar into a Right Side Seat position.

FINISHING POSITION
End in a Right Side Seat At End Mount position on the right bar. The right leg is vertically straight with the toes pointed downward. The left leg is bent with the upper leg from hip to knee sitting on the bar. The lower leg from knee to foot is angled toward the right knee with the left foot on top of the right knee. The back is straight and the head is level with the eyes focused forward. The right hand is gripping the bar behind the right buttocks and the left hand is gripping the other bar directly across from the left side of the body.

IMPORTANT TEACHING SUGGESTIONS

1) Take time in the introductory lesson to discuss the mechanics of the Right Side Seat At End Mount and follow-up with a demonstration of the mount by yourself or by a skilled student. If possible, reinforce the discussion and demonstration with a Right Side Seat At End Mount chart and/or a related audiovisual aid.

2) Take time in the introductory lesson to individually assess the proper execution of the mount and make necessary corrections, if needed.

3) Teach the Straight Arm Support (refer to page 78 for teaching guidelines) and Right Side Seat (refer to page 86 for teaching guidelines) as lead-up stunts to the Right Side Seat At End Mount.

4) Emphasize the need to perform the mount over a well matted area.

5) Stress the importance of using the overhand grip.

6) Make certain the students understand the importance of using a firm grip throughout the performance of the mount.

7) Stress the need to jump forward and upward to assume the proper momentary Straight Arm Support position above and between the ends of the bars.

8) After jumping, tell the students to push downward on the bars with force to help attain the proper momentary Straight Arm Support position above and between the ends of the bars.

9) Tell the students to swing the legs forward and upward after passing through the proper Straight Arm Support Position.

10) Emphasize the need to swing the legs high enough to pass above the bars.

11) Instruct the students to swing the legs over the right bar when the legs are slightly above the bars.

12) Discuss the "polished" look of the Right Side Seat At End Mount by having the right leg vertically straight with the toes pointed downward, left foot on the right knee, back straight, head level with the eyes focused forward, and the hands gripping the bars in their proper positions.

13) Assist students, if needed.

SPOTTING HINTS

Position yourself next to the end of the parallel bars while being directly beside the student's closest hand. Be on the side where the Right Side Seat At End Mount will be performed. Grasp the student's near wrist with your front hand and grasp the back of the student's closest upper arm near the student's arm pit with your back hand. The fingers of your back hand circle toward the front of the student's upper arm. On your signal, instruct the student to perform the Right Side Seat At End Mount. Give the student the necessary forward lift with your back hand to assume the proper momentary Straight Arm Support position at the end of the parallel bars. Continue to give the student the necessary support with your back hand to be able to maintain balance and stability while swinging the legs forward and upward to swing them sideward over the right bar. Once the student has attained the Right Side Seat position, give verbal cues to remind the student about the right leg being vertically straight with the toes pointed downward, left foot on the right knee, straight back, head level with the eyes focused forward, and proper hand positions on the bars. If possible, loosen your grips without losing physical contact in order to give the student some independence while performing the mount; however, be ready to tighten your grips if the student loses balance or begins to fall backward or sideward.

If the student can perform the first part of the mount and is able to assume the proper momentary Straight Arm Support position but has difficulty swinging the legs forward, upward, and over the bar, consider the following spotting modification. Maintain a strong, firm grip with your back hand on the student's upper arm, but release your grip on the student's wrist. Use your front hand to lift and guide the student's legs to help the student swing them over the right bar. Make certain you give the necessary lift and support with your back hand on the student's upper arm to keep the student in the proper balanced upright position.

Make certain you position yourself properly in both spotting techniques so as not to place undue pressure on your lower back or other potentially weak areas of your body. Do not overspot. Instead, have the student perform the Right Side Seat At End Mount by providing a minimum amount of spotting necessary to allow for a successful and safe performance of the mount. Continue to give individualized assistance using the preceding methods. If possible, encourage the student to practice the Right Side Seat At End Mount without assistance.

FORWARD ROLL INTO HAND KNEE HANG MOUNT

STARTING POSITION
Begin in a bent leg standing position at the side of the parallel bars with the heels off the mat so the weight is balanced above the balls of the feet. The arms are straight with the shoulders positioned directly in front of the near bar and the hands are in overhand grip positions on the bar. The head is level with the eyes focused forward.

PERFORMANCE
While maintaining a firm grip, jump forward and upward while pushing down on the bar to assume a balanced Straight Arm Support position against the side of the bar. The arms are straight and positioned along the sides of the body. The head is level and the body is diagonally straight up and down with the shoulders positioned directly above the hands. The hips are pressed against the bar and the toes are pointed downward. Bend at the waist while tucking the chin, rounding the back, bending the arms, and bending the legs. The body assumes a semi-tuck position. Do a semi-tuck forward roll over the bar and place the back of the legs (behind the knees) over the far bar to attain a cross bar Hand Knee Hang position.

FINISHING POSITION
End in a Forward Roll Into Hand Knee Hang Mount position with the legs, from knees to toes, hanging over the far bar. The toes are pointed diagonally downward. The arms are straight with the hands in overhand grip positions on the near bar. The hips are forward to create a slight arch in the back. The head is aligned with the body and the eyes are focused backward.

IMPORTANT TEACHING SUGGESTIONS

1) Take time in the introductory lesson to discuss the mechanics of the Forward Roll Into Hand Knee Hang Mount and follow-up with a demonstration of the mount by yourself or by a skilled student. If possible, reinforce the discussion and demonstration with a Forward Roll Into Hand Knee Hang Mount chart and/or a related audiovisual aid.

2) Take time in the introductory lesson to individually assess the proper execution of the mount and make necessary corrections, if needed.

3) Teach the Straight Arm Support At Side Mount (refer to page 61 for teaching guidelines) as the lead-up mount to the Forward Roll Into Hand Knee Hang Mount.

4) Emphasize the need to perform the mount above a well matted area.

5)   Stress the importance of using the overhand grip.

6)   Make certain the students understand the importance of using a firm grip throughout the performance of the mount.

7)   Stress the need to jump forward and upward to assume the proper Straight Arm Support position above and against the bar.

8)   After jumping, tell the students to push downward on the bar with force to help attain the proper Straight Arm Support Position above and against the bar.

9)   Stress the need to stop in a balanced Straight Arm Support position directly above and against the bar. The movements must be controlled so that balance is not lost resulting in the student falling forward or backward.

10)   Discuss the term balance and the role it plays when the body is against the bar in a Straight Arm Support position.

11)   Stress the need to bend slowly at the waist while tucking the chin, rounding the back, bending the arms, and bending the legs. These movements must be slow and completely under control.

12)   Caution the students about performing a semi-tuck forward roll over the bar so as not to strike the head on the far bar. It might be necessary for the students to tilt the head sideward to be able to safely perform the semi-tuck roll over the bar without the head striking the far bar.

13)   Explain how the hands turn on the bar while maintaining the overhand grip position throughout the performance of the mount.

14)   Tell the students to transfer the legs from the near bar to the far bar in a slow, controlled manner while maintaining a firm grip on the near bar.

15)   Discuss the "polished" look of the Hand Knee Hang by having the arms straight, the back slightly arched, the toes pointed diagonally downward, and the head properly aligned with the body.

16)   Assist the students, if necessary.

SPOTTING HINTS

Position yourself beside the parallel bars and facing the the student. Grasp the student's near wrist with your inside hand and grasp the back of the student's closest upper arm near the student's arm pit with your outside hand. The fingers of your outside hand circle toward the front of the student's upper arm. On your signal, instruct the student to perform the Forward Roll Into Hand Knee Hang Mount. Give the student the necessary forward lift with your outside hand to assume the proper Straight Arm Support position against the bar. After the student has assumed the proper Straight Arm Support position against the bar, release your grips. Then, grasp the student's near wrist with your outside hand. Use your inside hand to help the student bend at the waist into the proper semi-tuck position and begin the semi-tuck forward roll over the bar. Next, help guide the student's head with your inside hand during the semi-tuck forward roll so the student's head doesn't strike the far bar.

After the student has performed the semi-tuck forward roll, use the inside hand to help place the student's legs over the far bar to assume the Hand Knee Hang position.

Make certain you position yourself properly so as not to place undue pressure on your lower back or other potentially weak areas of your body. Do not overspot. Instead, have the student perform the Forward Roll Into Hand Knee Hang Mount by providing a minimum amount of spotting necessary to allow for a successful and safe performance of the mount. Continue to give individualized assistance using the preceding method. If possible, encourage the student to practice the Forward Roll Into Hand Knee Hang Mount without assistance.

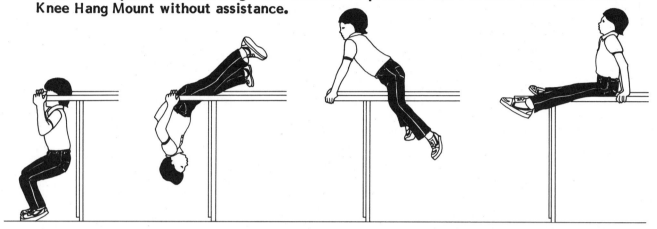

BACK PULL OVER INTO STRADDLE SEAT MOUNT

STARTING POSITION
Begin in a bent leg and straight back semi-standing backward position between the ends of the parallel bars. The hands are in an overhand grip around the outside ends of the bars. The arms are bent with the elbows directly below the hands. The head is level with the eyes focused forward.

PERFORMANCE
While maintaining a firm grip, push-off with the feet and pull upward with the arms to bring the knees to the chest while lifting the hips to begin the backward movement. At the same time, tuck the chin to the chest. Continue to pull upward and backward with the arms while lifting the hips between the bars. In the process, straighten the legs so the legs point diagonally backward, sideward, and upward between and slightly above the bars. When the hips are positioned between the bars, straddle the legs so the outside of the upper thighs press against the inside of the bars. At the same time, start to lift the head and upper body while moving the hands around the ends of the bars. When the head and upper body pass between the bars, begin to push downward on the bars to allow the legs to roll on the top of the bars. The legs remain in the straddle leg position. Continue to push downward on the ends of the bars while lifting the head and upper body to start to assume a Straddle Seat position on top of the bars. Release the grips and sit back while swinging the legs forward and upward to attain a Straddle Seat position. Grip the bars beside the buttocks.

FINISHING POSITION
End in a Back Pull Over Into Straddle Seat Mount position on top of the bars with the legs straight and the toes pointed diagonally sideward. The back is straight and the head is level with the eyes focused forward. The hands are gripping the bars beside the buttocks.

IMPORTANT TEACHING SUGGESTIONS

1) Take time in the introductory lesson to discuss the mechanics of the Back Pull Over Into Straddle Seat Mount and follow-up with a demonstration of the mount by yourself or by a skilled student. If possible, reinforce the discussion and demonstration with a Back Pull Over Into Straddle Seat Mount chart and/or a related audiovisual aid.

2) Take time in the introductory lesson to individually assess the proper execution of the mount and make necessary corrections, if needed.

3) Teach the Birds Nest (refer to page 104 for teaching guidelines) and the Straddle Seat (refer to page 83 for teaching guidelines) as lead-up stunts to the Back Pull Over Into Straddle Seat Mount.

4) Emphasize the need to perform the mount above a well matted area.

5) Stress the importance of using the overhand grip.

6) Make certain the students understand the importance of using a firm grip throughout the performance of the mount.

7) Explain why it is advantageous to begin the mount with the arms bent rather than to have the arms straight. By having the arms bent, the shoulders are closer to the bars. This permits more efficient use of the muscles in the arms, shoulders, chest, and upper back to help maneuver the body.

8) Emphasize the need to pull upward and backward with the arms to position the hips between the bars so the legs can separate into the straddle leg position.

9) Tell the students to press the outside of the upper legs against the inside of the bars with great force to assist the lifting of the head and upper body.

10) Make certain the students know and understand the importance of moving the hands around the ends of the bars throughout the performance of the mount.

11) After the shoulders pass between the bars, discuss the need to push downward on the ends of the bars with the hands to help lift the head and upper body while rolling across the bars on the front of the thighs to assume the Straddle Seat position.

12) Caution the students about being in a balanced semi-upright straddle leg position before releasing the grips to swing the legs forward and upward to assume the Straddle Seat position. If the grip release is too early, the student may lose balance and fall forward instead of continuing the backward movement.

13) Suggest a downward push on the ends of the bars prior to releasing the grips to give additional backward momentum to help attain the Straddle Seat position.

14) Discuss the "polished" look of the Back Pull Over Into Straddle Seat Mount by having the legs straight with the toes pointed diagonally sideward. Also, the back is straight and the head is level with the eyes focused forward. The hands grip the bars beside the buttocks.

15) Assist students, if necessary.

SPOTTING HINTS

Position yourself next to the end of the parallel bars while being beside the student at his/her level. Depending on your height and the height of the parallel bars, you will be positioned in a kneeling, squatting, or bent leg straddle position. Grasp the student's closest wrist with your back hand. On your signal, instruct the student to perform the Back Pull Over Into Straddle Seat Mount. Use your front hand to assist the upward and backward movements. In the beginning, assistance can be given by placing your front hand behind the student's closest knee to give additional lift and power to the initial upward and backward movements. Remove your hand as soon as the student has positioned his/her hips between the bars and is ready to extend the legs diagonally backward, sideward, and upward between and slightly above the bars. Maintain your grip on the student's closest wrist with your back hand. Place your front hand on top of the student's closest shoulder. Use your front hand to help the student lift his/her head and upper body while the student's legs roll across the top of the bars. Also, reposition yourself to be at an appropriate level to continue the spotting process. When the student is ready to release his/her grip to swing the legs forward and upward to assume the Straddle Seat position, let go of the student's closest wrist. Prior to releasing the grip of your back hand, reposition your front hand by grasping the front of the student's closest upper arm near the student's arm pit. The fingers of your front hand circle toward the back of the student's upper arm. Use your front hand to help the student continue the backward movement to attain the Straddle Seat position. As soon as the student grips the bars beside the buttocks, grasp the student's closest wrist with your back hand. Once the student assumes the Straddle Seat position, give verbal cues to remind the student about straight legs, pointed toes, straight back, and head level with the eyes focused forward.

Make certain you position yourself properly during the entire spotting process so as not to place undue pressure on your lower back or other potentially weak areas of your body. Do not overspot. Instead, have the student perform the Back Pull Over Into Straddle Seat Mount by providing a minimum amount of spotting necessary to allow for a successful and safe performance of the mount. Continue to give individualized assistance using the preceding method. If possible, encourage the student to practice the Back Pull Over Into Straddle Seat Mount without assistance.

Chapter – 5

STUNTS

INTRODUCTION

The Stunts Chapter includes a detailed explanation of nineteen parallel bars stunts. Each explanation includes three phases: Starting Position, Performance, and Finishing Position. In addition, each parallel bars stunt has a list of Important Teaching Suggestions and a Spotting Hints section.

STRAIGHT ARM SUPPORT

STARTING POSITION
Stand in the middle of the parallel bars.
Use an overhand grip to grasp the bars.

PERFORMANCE
While maintaining a firm grip, jump
upward while pushing down on the bars
to assume a balanced Straight Arm Support position above and between the bars.

FINISHING POSITION
End in a Straight Arm Support position. The arms are straight and positioned along the sides of the body. The head is level and the body is straight up and down with the shoulders positioned directly above the hands. The toes are pointed downward.

IMPORTANT TEACHING SUGGESTIONS

1) Take time in the introductory lesson to discuss the mechanics of the Straight Arm Support and follow-up with a demonstration of the stunt by yourself or by a skilled student. If possible, reinforce the discussion and demonstration with a Straight Arm Support chart and/or a related audiovisual aid.

2) Take time in the introductory lesson to individually assess the proper execution of the stunt and make necessary corrections, if needed.

3) Emphasize the need to perform the stunt above a well matted area.

4) Have the students perform the stunt at the center of the parallel bars until the stunt as been mastered.

5) Stress the importance of using the overhand grip.

6) Make certain the students understand the importance of using a firm grip throughout the performance of the stunt.

7) Discuss the need to jump directly upward to assume the proper Straight Arm Support position above and between the bars.

8) After jumping, tell the students to push downward on the bars with force to help attain the proper Straight Arm Support position above and between the bars.

9) Stress the importance of keeping the shoulders directly above the hands throughout the performance of the stunt while keeping the head level and the body in a straight up and down position.

10) Encourage smooth movements with minimum swinging of the body during the performance of the stunt.

11) Assist students, if necessary.

SPOTTING HINTS

Position yourself next to the parallel bars while being directly beside the student's closest hand. Grasp the student's near wrist with your front hand and grasp the back of the student's closest upper arm near the student's arm pit with your back hand. The fingers of your back hand circle toward the front of the student's upper arm. On your signal, instruct the student to perform the Straight Arm Support. Give the student the necessary lift with your back hand to assume the proper or modified Straight Arm Support position above and between the bars. If the student achieves the proper Straight Arm Support position, loosen your grips without losing physical contact in order to give the student some independence while performing the stunt; however, be ready to tighten your grips if the student is unable to balance and/or support his/her body in the proper Straight Arm Support position. Make certain you position yourself properly so as not to place undue pressure on your lower back or other potentially weak areas of your body. Do not overspot. Instead, have the student perform the Straight Arm Support by providing a minimum amount of spotting necessary to allow for a successful and safe performance of the stunt. Continue to give individualized assistance using the preceding method. If possible, encourage the student to practice the Straight Arm Support without assistance.

STRAIGHT ARM SUPPORT DIP

STARTING POSITION
Begin in a Straight Arm Support position at the center of the parallel bars.

PERFORMANCE
While maintaining a firm grip, bend the arms slowly to lower the body until the elbow joint is slightly less than at a right angle. The shoulders pass in front of the elbows and they become positioned above but a little in front of the hands. The body, from head to toes, has tilted slightly forward and backward to compensate for the new position of the shoulders. Push down on the hands with sufficient upper body force to lift the body to return to the original upright position.

FINISHING POSITION
End in a Straight Arm Support position at the center of the parallel bars.

IMPORTANT TEACHING SUGGESTIONS

1)   Take time in the introductory lesson to discuss the mechanics of the Straight Arm Support Dip and follow-up with a demonstration of the stunt by yourself or by a skilled student. If possible, reinforce the discussion and demonstration with a Straight Arm Support Dip chart and/or a related audiovisual aid.

2)   Take time in the introductory lesson to individually assess the proper execution of the stunt and make necessary corrections, if needed.

3)   Teach the Straight Arm Support (refer to page 78 for teaching guidelines) as the lead-up stunt to the Straight Arm Support Dip.

4)   <u>Do not</u> permit a student to attempt a Straight Arm Support Dip until the student has successfully mastered the Straight Arm Support position.

5)   Emphasize the need to perform the stunt above a well matted area.

6)   Have the students perform the stunt at the center of the parallel bars until the stunt has been mastered.

7)   Stress the importance of using the overhand grip.

8)   Make certain the students understand the importance of using a firm grip throughout the performance of the stunt.

9)   Stress the need to bend the arms slowly in order to safely lower the body.

10)   Discuss upper body and arm strength and the need to have it in order to be successful to push downward on the hands to lift the body to its original position.

11)   Talk about the major muscle groups located in the upper body and arms that are used to lift the body to its original upright position. Use audiovisual materials, if possible.

12)   Assist students, if necessary.

SPOTTING HINTS

Position yourself next to the parallel bars while being slightly behind and to the side of the student. Grasp the student's near wrist with your front hand and grasp the back of the student's closest upper arm near the student's arm pit with your back hand. The fingers of your back hand circle toward the front of the student's upper arm. On your signal, instruct the student to perform the Straight Arm Support Dip. Give the student the necessary support and lift with your back hand to be able to maintain balance and be able to lower then lift the body. If possible, loosen your grips without losing physical contact in order to give the student some independence while performing the stunt; however, be ready to tighten your grips if the student loses balance or is unable to support and lift the body. Make certain you position yourself properly so as not to place undue pressure on your lower back or other potentially weak areas of your body. <u>Do not</u> overspot. Instead, have the student perform the Straight Arm Support Dip by providing a minimum amount of spotting necessary to allow for a successful and safe performance of the stunt. Continue to give individualized assistance using the preceding methods. If possible, encourage the student to practice the Straight Arm Support Dip without assistance.

VARIATION

Challenge advanced skill level students to perform a series of continuous Straight Arm Support Dips. Begin with two and increase the number by one each time success is met at the previous number.

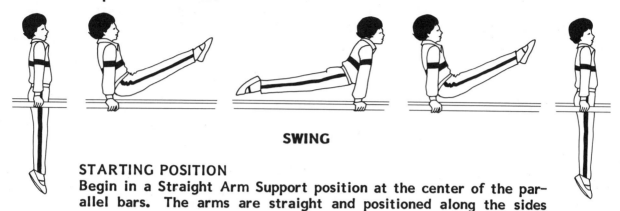

SWING

STARTING POSITION
Begin in a Straight Arm Support position at the center of the parallel bars. The arms are straight and positioned along the sides of the body. The head is level and the body is straight up and down with the shoulders positioned directly above the hands. The toes are pointed downward.

PERFORMANCE
While maintaining a firm grip, lift the legs and feet in front of the body while bending at the waist. Swing the legs and feet downward, backward, and upward to assume an arch position. Swing the legs and feet downward and forward to position the legs and feet in front of the body while bending at the waist. Keep the arms locked and the shoulders positioned directly above the hands throughout the entire performance of the Swing. Make the shoulders the fulcrum of the Swing.

FINISHING POSITION
End in a Straight Arm Support position at the center of the parallel bars. The arms are straight and positioned along the sides of the body. The head is level and the body is straight up and down with the shoulders positioned directly above the hands. The toes are pointed downward.

IMPORTANT TEACHING SUGGESTIONS

1) Take time in the introductory lesson to discuss the mechanics of the Swing and follow-up with a demonstration of the stunt by yourself or by a skilled student. If possible, reinforce the discussion and demonstration with a Swing chart and/or a related audiovisual aid.

2) Take time in the introductory lesson to individually assess the proper execution of the stunt and make necessary corrections, if needed.

3) Teach the Straight Arm Support (refer to page 78 for teaching guidelines) as the lead-up stunt to the Swing.

4) Do not permit a student to attempt a Swing until the student has successfully mastered the Straight Arm Support position.

5) Emphasize the need to perform the stunt above a well matted area.

6) Have the students perform the stunt at the center of the parallel bars until the stunt has been mastered.

7)   Stress the importance of using the overhand grip.

8)   Make certain the students understand the importance of using a firm grip throughout the performance of the stunt.

9)   Stress the need to keep the arms locked and the shoulders directly above the hands throughout the performance of the stunt.

10)   Discuss the term "fulcrum" and relate it to the position of the shoulders throughout the performance of the stunt.

11)   Tell the students to bend at the waist as the legs and feet swing forward and upward to assume the pike position.

12)   Discuss the term "balance" and relate it to the equal swinging motion of the legs and feet in front of and in back of the body.

13)   Tell the students to keep the toes pointed throughout the performance of the stunt.

14)   Assist students, if necessary.

SPOTTING HINTS

Position yourself next to the parallel bars while being slightly behind and to the side of the student. Grasp the student's near wrist with your front hand and grasp the back of the student's closest upper arm near the student's arm pit with your back hand. The fingers of your back hand circle toward the front of the student's upper arm. On your signal, instruct the student to perform the Swing. Give the student the necessary support with your back hand to be able to maintain balance and stability while swinging the legs and feet forward and backward. If possible, loosen your grips without losing physical contact in order to give the student some independence while performing the stunt; however, be ready to tighten your grips if the student loses balance or begins to fall forward or backward. Make certain you position yourself properly so as not to place undue pressure on your lower back or other potentially weak areas of your body. Do not overspot. Instead, have the student perform the Swing by providing a minimum amount of spotting necessary to allow for a successful and safe performance of the stunt. Continue to give individualized assistance using the preceding method. If possible, encourage the student to practice the Swing without assistance.

VARIATIONS

1)   Challenge advanced skill level students to continue to swing the legs and feet backward and forward a number of times prior to finishing in the Straight Arm Support position.

2)   Challenge advanced skill level students to gradually increase the height of the forward and backward swings.

3)   Teach advanced skill level students to keep the hips aligned with the abdomen and legs so the body is extended forward in a slightly arched position during the forward swing instead of creating a pike position.

STRADDLE SEAT

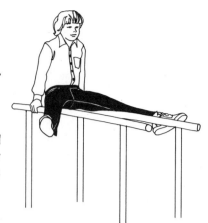

STARTING POSITION
Begin in a Straight Arm Support position at the center of the parallel bars.

PERFORMANCE
While maintaining a firm grip, lift the legs forward and upward between the bars. As the legs pass slightly above the bars, separate them and place one leg across each bar.

FINISHING POSITION
End in a Straddle Seat position on top of the bars with the legs straight and the toes pointed diagonally sideward. The back is straight and the head is level with the eyes focused forward. The hands are gripping the bars beside the buttocks.

IMPORTANT TEACHING SUGGESTIONS

1) Take time in the introductory lesson to discuss the mechanics of the Straddle Seat and follow-up with a demonstration of the stunt by yourself or by a skilled student. If possible, reinforce the discussion and demonstration with a Straddle Seat chart and/or a related audiovisual aid.

2) Take time in the introductory lesson to individually assess the proper execution of the stunt and make necessary corrections, if needed.

3) Teach the Straight Arm Support (refer to page 78 for teaching guidelines) as the lead-up stunt to the Straddle Seat.

4) Emphasize the need to perform the stunt above a well matted area.

5) Have the students perform the stunt at the center of the parallel bars until the stunt has been mastered.

6) Stress the importance of using the overhand grip.

7) Make certain the students understand the importance of using a firm grip throughout the performance of the stunt.

8) Tell the students to lift the legs forward and upward high enough to pass above the bars.

9) Instruct the students to separate the legs quickly when the legs are slightly above the bars.

10) Discuss the "polished" look of the Straddle Seat by having the legs straight with the toes pointed diagonally sideward, back straight, head level with the eyes focused forward, and the hands gripping the bars beside the buttocks.

11) Assist the students, if necessary.

SPOTTING HINTS

Position yourself next to the parallel bars while being slightly behind and to the side of the student. Grasp the student's near wrist with your front hand and grasp the back of the student's closest upper arm near the student's arm pit with your back hand. The fingers of your back hand circle toward the front of the student's upper arm. On your signal, instruct the student to perform the Straddle Seat. Give the student the necessary support with your back hand to be able to maintain balance and stability while lifting the legs forward and upward to place them on the bars. Once the legs are on the bars, give verbal cues to remind the student about straight legs, pointed toes, straight back, head level with the eyes focused forward, and proper hand positions on the bars. If possible, loosen your grips without losing physical contact in order to give the student some independence while performing the stunt; however, be ready to tighten the grips if the student loses balance or begins to fall forward or backward.

If the student can perform the Straight Arm Support but has difficulty lifting the legs forward and upward to pass slightly above the bars, consider the following spotting modification: Maintain a strong, firm grip with your back hand on the student's upper arm, but release your grip on the student's wrist. Use your front hand to lift and guide the student's closest leg to help place it on top of the near bar. Most of the time, the student is able to place the far leg on the far bar at the same time or a little behind the placement of the near leg on the near bar. Make certain you give the necessary lift and support with your back hand on the student's upper arm to keep the student in the proper balanced upright position.

Make certain you position yourself properly in both spotting techniques so as not to place undue pressure on your lower back or other potentially weak areas of your body. <u>Do not</u> overspot. Instead, have the student perform the Straddle Seat by providing a minimum amount of spotting necessary to allow for a successful and safe performance of the stunt. Continue to give individualized assistance using one of the preceding methods. If possible, encourage the student to practice the Straddle Seat without assistance.

LEFT SIDE SEAT

STARTING POSITION
Begin in a Straight Arm Support position at the center of the parallel bars.

PERFORMANCE
While maintaining a firm grip, lift the legs forward and upward between the bars. As the legs pass slightly above the bars, swing them sideward over the left bar and assume a side seat position.

FINISHING POSITION
End in a Left Side Seat position on the left bar. The left leg is vertically straight with the toes pointed downward. The right leg is bent with the upper leg from hip to knee sitting on the bar. The lower leg from knee to foot is angled toward the left knee with the right foot on top of the left knee. The back is straight and the head is level with the eyes focused forward. The left hand is gripping the bar behind the left buttocks and the right hand is gripping the other bar directly across from the right side of the body.

IMPORTANT TEACHING SUGGESTIONS

1) Take time in the introductory lesson to discuss the mechanics of the Left Side Seat and follow-up with a demonstration of the stunt by yourself or by a skilled student. If possible, reinforce the discussion and demonstration with a Left Side Seat chart and/or a related audiovisual aid.

2) Take time in the introductory lesson to individually assess the proper execution of the stunt and make necessary corrections, if needed.

3) Teach the Straight Arm Support (refer to page 78 for teaching guidelines) as the lead-up stunt to the Left Side Seat.

4) Emphasize the need to perform the stunt above a well matted area.

5) Have the students perform the stunt at the center of the parallel bars until the stunt has been mastered.

6) Stress the importance of using the overhand grip.

7) Make certain the students understand the importance of using a firm grip throughout the performance of the stunt.

8) Tell the students to lift the legs forward and upward high enough to pass above the bars.

9) Instruct the students to swing the legs over the left bar when the legs are slightly above the bars.

10) Discuss the "polished" look of the Left Side Seat by having the left leg vertically straight with the toes pointed downward, right foot on the left knee, back straight, head level with the eyes focused forward, and the hands gripping the bars in their proper positions.

11) Assist students, if necessary.

SPOTTING HINTS

Position yourself next to the parallel bars while being slightly behind and to the side of the student. Be on the side where the Left Side Seat will be performed. Grasp the student's near wrist with your front hand and grasp the back of the student's closest upper arm near the student's arm pit with your back hand. The fingers of your back hand circle toward the front of the student's upper arm. On your signal, instruct the student to perform the Left Side Seat. Give the student the necessary support with your back hand to be able to maintain balance and stability while lifting the legs forward and upward to swing them over the near bar to assume the Left Side Seat position. Once the student is in the Left Side Seat position, give verbal cues to remind the student about the left leg being vertically straight with the toes pointed downward, right foot on the left knee, straight back, head level with the eyes focused forward, and proper hand positions on the bars. If possible, loosen your grips without losing physical contact in order to give the student some independence while performing the stunt; however, be ready to tighten your grips if the student loses balance or begins to fall backward or sideward.

If the student can perform the Straight Arm Support but has difficulty lifting the legs forward and upward to swing them over the bar, consider the following spotting modification: Maintain a strong, firm grip with your back hand on the student's upper arm, but release your grip on the student's wrist. Use your front hand to lift and guide the student's legs to help the student swing them over the near bar. Make certain you give the necessary lift and support with your back hand on the student's upper arm to keep the student in the proper balanced upright position.

Make certain you position yourself properly in both spotting techniques so as not to place undue pressure on your lower back or other potentially weak areas of your body. <u>Do not</u> overspot. Instead, have the student perform the Left Side Seat by providing a minimum amount of spotting necessary to allow for a successful and safe performance of the stunt. Continue to give individualized assistance using one of the preceding methods. If possible, encourage the student to practice the Left Side Seat without assistance.

VARIATION

Teach advanced skill level students to release their grips after they have assumed the proper Left Side Seat position on the bar. Have them lift the arms and extend the arms sideward at shoulder level with the fingers together and straight.

RIGHT SIDE SEAT

STARTING POSITION
Begin in a Straight Arm Support position at the center of the parallel bars.

PERFORMANCE
While maintaining a firm grip, lift the legs forward and upward between the bars. As the legs pass slightly above the bars, swing them sideward over the right bar and assume a side seat position.

FINISHING POSITION
End in a Right Side Seat position on the right bar. The right leg is vertically straight with the toes pointed downward. The left leg is bent with the upper leg from hip to knee sitting on the bar. The lower leg from knee to foot is angled toward the right knee with the left foot on top of the right knee. The back is straight and the head is level with the eyes focused forward. The right hand is gripping the bar behind the right buttocks and the left hand is gripping the other bar directly across from the left side of the body.

IMPORTANT TEACHING SUGGESTIONS

1)   Take time in the introductory lesson to discuss the mechanics of the Right Side Seat and follow-up with a demonstration of the stunt by yourself or by a skilled student. If possible, reinforce the discussion and demonstration with a Right Side Seat chart and/or a related audiovisual aid.

2) Take time in the introductory lesson to individually assess the proper execution of the stunt and make necessary corrections, if needed.

3) Teach the Straight Arm Support (refer to page 78 for teaching guidelines) as the lead-up to the Right Side Seat.

4) Emphasize the need to perform the stunt above a well matted area.

5) Have the students perform the stunt at the center of the parallel bars until the stunt as been mastered.

6) Stress the importance of using the overhand grip.

7) Make certain the students understand the importance of using a firm grip throughout the performance of the stunt.

8) Tell the students to lift the legs forward and upward high enough to pass above the bars.

9) Instruct the students to swing the legs over the right bar when the legs are slightly above the bars.

10) Discuss the "polished" look of the Right Side Seat by having the right leg vertically straight with the toes pointed downward, left foot on the right knee, back straight, head level with the eyes focused forward, and the hands gripping the bars in their proper positions.

11) Assist students, if necessary.

SPOTTING HINTS

Position yourself next to the parallel bars while being slightly behind and to the side of the student. Be on the side where the Right Side Seat will be performed. Grasp the student's near wrist with your front hand and grasp the back of the student's closest upper arm near the student's armpit with your back hand. The fingers of your back hand circle toward the front of the student's upper arm. On your signal, instruct the student to perform the Right Side Seat. Give the student the necessary support with your back hand to be able to maintain balance and stability while lifting the legs forward and upward to swing them over the near bar to assume the Right Side Seat position. Once the student is in the Right Side Seat position, give verbal cues to remind the student about the right leg being vertically straight with the toes pointed downward, left foot on the right knee, straight back, head level with the eyes focused forward, and proper hand positions on the bars. If possible, loosen your grips without losing physical contact in order to give the student some independence while performing the stunt; however, be ready to tighten your grips if the student loses balance or begins to fall backward or sideward.

If the student can perform the Straight Arm Support but has difficulty lifting the legs forward and upward to swing them over the bar, consider the following spotting modification: Maintain a strong, firm grip with your back hand on the student's upper arm, but release your grip on the student's wrist. Use your front hand to lift and guide the student's legs to help the student swing them over the near bar. Make certain you give the necessary lift and support with your back hand on the student's upper arm to keep the student in the proper balanced upright position.

Make certain you position yourself properly in both spotting techniques so as not to place undue pressure on your lower back or other potentially weak areas of your body. Do not overspot. Instead, have the student perform the Right Side Seat by providing a minimum amount of spotting necessary to allow for a successful and safe performance of the stunt. Continue to give individualized assistance using one of the preceding methods. If possible, encourage the student to perform the Right Side Seat without assistance.

VARIATION

Teach advanced skill level students to release their grips after they have assumed the proper Right Side Seat position on the bar. Have them lift the arms and extend the arms sideward at shoulder level with the fingers together and straight.

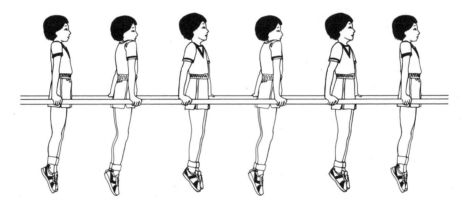

HAND WALK FORWARD

STARTING POSITION
Begin in a Forward Straight Arm Support position near the beginning of the parallel bars.

PERFORMANCE
While maintaining a firm grip, walk forward with the hands the length of the parallel bars or as far as possible keeping the body in a Straight Arm Support position. When traveling, keep the arms locked, head level, and the body straight up and down with the legs and feet together and the toes pointed downward. As one hand leaves the bar to take a step, shift the body weight to the other hand. Take small steps with the hands.

FINISHING POSITION
End in a Straight Arm Support position near the end of the parallel bars or at a lesser distance depending upon how far one was able to travel.

IMPORTANT TEACHING SUGGESTIONS

1) Take time in the introductory lesson to discuss the mechanics of the Hand Walk Forward and follow-up with a demonstration of the stunt by yourself or by a skilled student. If possible, reinforce the discussion and demonstration with a Hand Walk Forward chart and/or a related audiovisual aid.

2) Take time in the introductory lesson to individually assess the proper execution of the stunt and make necessary corrections, if needed.

3) Teach the Straight Arm Support (refer to page 78 for teaching guidelines) as the lead-up stunt to the Hand Walk Forward.

4) Do not permit a student to attempt the Hand Walk Forward until the student has successfully mastered the Straight Arm Support position.

5) Emphasize the need to perform the stunt above a well matted area.

6) Stress the importance of using the overhand grip.

7) Make certain the students understand the importance of using firm grips throughout the performance of the stunt.

8) Discuss the importance of keeping the arms locked throughout the performance of the stunt.

9) Emphasize the need to keep the legs and feet together to help control the swinging and swaying of the body as it travels forward between the parallel bars.

10) Explain the need to shift the body weight to the support hand during the time the other hand leaves the bar to take a step.

11) Make certain the students take small steps with the hands.

12) Discuss upper body and arm strength and the need to have it in order to be successful in performing the stunt.

13) Talk about the major muscle groups in the upper body and arms that are used to help propel the body forward during the performance of the stunt.

14) Assist students, if necessary.

SPOTTING HINTS

Position yourself next to the parallel bars while being slightly behind and to the side of the student. Grasp the back of the student's closest upper arm near the student's arm pit with your back hand and grasp the front of the student's closest upper arm below your back hand with your front hand. The fingers of your back hand circle toward the front of the upper arm and the fingers of your front hand circle toward the back of the upper arm. On your signal, instruct the student to perform the Hand Walk Forward. Give the student the necessary support and lift to be able to maintain balance and be capable of moving the body forward in the proper Hand Walk Forward position. Move forward with the student by repositioning yourself. If possible, loosen your grips without losing physical contact in order to give the student some independence while performing the stunt; however, be ready to tighten your grips if the student is unable to support, lift, and/or maintain balance of the body. Make certain you position yourself properly so as not to place undue pressure on your lower back or other potentially weak areas of your body. Do not overspot. Instead, have the student perform the Hand Walk Forward by providing a minimum amount of spotting necessary to allow for a successful and safe performance of the stunt. Continue to give individualized assistance using the preceding method. If possible, encourage the student to practice the Hand Walk Forward without assistance.

VARIATION

Challenge advanced skill level students to perform the Hand Walk Forward to the far end of the parallel bars then perform the Straight Arm Support Turn (refer to page 112 for teaching guidelines) to return to the original starting position or to a lesser distance depending upon how far one was able to travel by repeating the Hand Walk Forward.

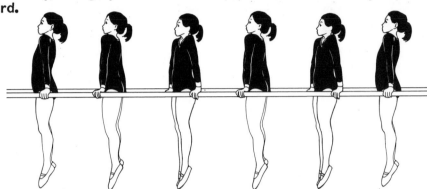

HAND WALK BACKWARD

STARTING POSITION
Begin in a backward Straight Arm Support position near the beginning of the parallel bars.

PERFORMANCE
While maintaining a firm grip, walk backward with the hands to a predetermined stopping point on the parallel bars, marked with tape, keeping the body in a Straight Arm Support position. When traveling, keep the arms locked, head level, and the body straight up and down with the legs and feet together and the toes pointed downward. Make certain the predetermined stopping point on the parallel bars is a safe distance from the end of the parallel bars. Do not allow students to Hand Walk Backward to the end of the parallel bars. As one hand leaves the bar to take a step, shift the body weight to the other hand. Take small steps with the hands.

FINISHING POSITION
End in a backward Straight Arm Support position at the predetermined stopping point on the parallel bars or at a lesser distance depending upon how far one was able to travel.

IMPORTANT TEACHING SUGGESTIONS

1)   Take time in the introductory lesson to discuss the mechanics of the Hand Walk Backward and follow-up with a demonstration of the stunt by yourself or by a skilled student. If possible, reinforce the discussion and demonstration with a Hand Walk Backward chart and/or a related audiovisual aid.

2)   Take time in the introductory lesson to individually assess the proper execution of the stunt and make necessary corrections, if needed.

3)   Teach the Straight Arm Support (refer to page 78 for teaching guidelines) as the lead-up stunt to the Hand Walk Backward.

4)   Do not permit a student to attempt the Hand Walk Backward until the student has successfully mastered the Straight Arm Support position.

5) Emphasize the need to perform the stunt above a well matted area.

6) Stress the importance of using the overhand grip.

7) Make certain the students understand the importance of using firm grips throughout the performance of the stunt.

8) Discuss the importance of keeping the arms locked throughout the performance of the stunt.

9) Emphasize the need to keep the legs and feet together to help control the swinging and swaying of the body as it travels backward between the parallel bars.

10) Explain the need to shift the body weight to the support hand during the time the other hand leaves the bar to take a step.

11) Make certain the students take small steps with the hands.

12) Do not allow students to hand walk backward to the end of the parallel bars. Use tape to mark the predetermined stopping point on the parallel bars a safe distance from the end of the parallel bars.

12) Discuss upper body and arm strength and the need to have it in order to be successful in performing the stunt.

13) Talk about the major muscle groups in the upper body and arms that are used to help propel the body backward during the performance of the stunt.

14) Assist students, if necessary.

SPOTTING HINTS

Position yourself next to the parallel bars while being slightly behind and to the side of the student. Grasp the back of the student's closest upper arm near the student's arm pit with your front hand and grasp the front of the student's closest upper arm below your front hand with your back hand. The fingers of your front hand circle toward the front of the student's upper arm and the fingers of your back hand circle toward the back of the student's upper arm. On your signal, instruct the student to perform the Hand Walk Backward. Give the student the necessary support and lift to be able to maintain balance and be capable to move the body backward in the proper Hand Walk Backward position. Move backward with the student by repositioning yourself. If possible, loosen your grips without losing physical contact in order to give the student some independence while performing the stunt; however, be ready to tighten your grips if the student is unable to support, lift, and/or maintain balance of the body. Make certain you position yourself properly so as not to place undue pressure on your lower back or other potentially weak areas of your body. Do not overspot. Instead, have the student perform the Hand Walk Backward by providing a minimum amount of spotting necessary to allow for a successful and safe performance of the stunt. Continue to give individualized assistance using the preceding method. If possible, encourage the student to practice the Hand Walk Backward without assistance.

VARIATION

Challenge advanced skill level students to perform the Hand Walk Backward to the predetermined stopping point then perform the Straight Arm Support Turn (refer to page 112 for teaching guidelines) to return to a safe stopping point, marked with tape, or to a lesser distance depending upon how far one was able to travel by repeating the Hand Walk Backward.

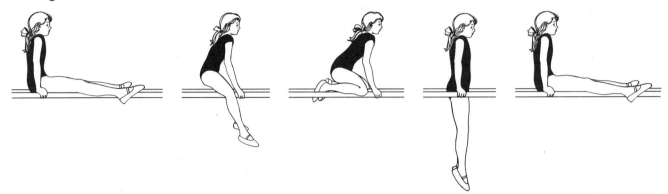

TRAVELING STRADDLE SEAT

STARTING POSITION
Begin in a Straddle Seat position near the beginning of the parallel bars.

PERFORMANCE
Release the grip and begin to lean forward while allowing the legs to swing downward. Place the hands on the parallel bars in front of and between the legs. Keep the arms straight. When the shoulders are positioned above the hands, lift the legs backward and upward to place them on top of the parallel bars to assume a Crouch Position. Next, lower the legs and feet between the bars to place the body in a Straight Arm Support position then immediately lift the legs forward and upward between the bars. As the legs pass slightly above the bars, separate them and place one leg across each bar.

FINISHING POSITION
End in a Straddle Seat position near the center of the parallel bars.

IMPORTANT TEACHING SUGGESTIONS

1) Take time in the introductory lesson to discuss the mechanics of the Traveling Straddle Seat and follow-up with a demonstration of the stunt by yourself or by a skilled student. If possible, reinforce the discussion and demonstration with a Traveling Straddle Seat chart and/or a related audiovisual aid.

2) Take time in the introductory lesson to individually assess the proper execution of the stunt and make necessary corrections, if needed.

3) Teach the Straddle Seat (refer to page 83 for teaching guidelines) as the lead-up stunt to the Traveling Straddle Seat.

4) Emphasize the need to perform the stunt above a well matted area.

5) Stress the importance of using the overhand grip.

6)   Make certain the students understand the importance of using firm grips throughout the performance of the stunt.

7)   Discuss the need to keep the arms locked throughout the performance of the stunt.

8)   Explain the need to position the shoulders above the hands before lifting the legs backward and upward to place them on top of the parallel bars. Then, keep the shoulders above the hands as the legs and feet are lowered between the bars into the Straight Arm Support position and while the legs are lifted forward and upward to return to the Straddle Seat position.

9)   Tell the students to lift the legs forward and upward high enough to pass above the bars.

10)   Instruct the students to separate the legs quickly when the legs are slightly above the bars.

11)   Make certain the students start the stunt near the beginning of the parallel bars.

12)   Assist students, if necessary.

SPOTTING HINTS

Position yourself next to the parallel bars while being slightly in front of and to the side of the student. On your signal, instruct the student to perform the Traveling Straddle Seat. As the student places the hands on the parallel bars in front of and between the legs, grasp the student's near wrist with your front hand and grasp the back of the student's closest upper arm near the student's arm pit with your back hand. The fingers of your back hand circle toward the front of the student's upper arm. Give the student the necessary support with your back hand to be able to maintain balance and stability while lowering the legs and feet between the bars and while lifting the legs forward and upward to place them on the bars. If possible, loosen your grips without losing physical contact in order to give the student some independence while performing the stunts; however, be ready to tighten your grips if the student loses balance or begins to fall forward or backward. Make certain you position yourself properly so as not to place undue pressure on your lower back or other potentially weak areas of your body. Do not overspot. Instead, have the student perform the Traveling Straddle Seat by providing a minimum amount of spotting necessary to allow for a successful and safe performance of the stunt. Continue to give individualized assistance using the preceding method. If possible, encourage the student to practice the Traveling Straddle Seat without assistance.

VARIATIONS

1)   Challenge advanced skill level students to perform a series of Traveling Straddle Seats starting at the beginning of the parallel bars and stopping near the end of the parallel bars.

2)   Teach advanced skill level students to perform the Traveling Straddle Seat by keeping the legs straight with toes pointed throughout the entire performance

of the stunt. The Crouch Position is eliminated as the legs are lifted behind the student prior to swinging them downward then upward to be placed on the parallel bars.

CROUCH POSITION

STARTING POSITION
Begin in a Straddle Seat position at the center of the parallel bars.

PERFORMANCE
Release the grip and begin to lean forward while allowing the legs to swing downward. Place the hands on the parallel bars in front of and between the legs.
Keep the arms straight. When the shoulders are positioned above the hands, lift the legs backward and upward to place them on top of the parallel bars.

FINISHING POSITION
End in a Crouch Position. The hands grip the bars a comfortable distance in front of the lower thighs and knees. The knees are positioned on the outside of the bars with the lower legs crossing diagonally over the bars so the feet are inside the bars. The toes are pointed diagonally backward. The head is level with the eyes focused forward.

IMPORTANT TEACHING SUGGESTIONS

1) Take time in the introductory lesson to discuss the mechanics of the Crouch Position and follow-up with a demonstration of the stunt by yourself or by a skilled student. If possible, reinforce the discussion and demonstration with a Crouch Position chart and/or a related audiovisual aid.

2) Take time in the introductory lesson to individually assess the proper execution of the stunt and make necessary corrections, if needed.

3) Teach the Straddle Seat (refer to page 83 for teaching guidelines) as the lead-up stunt to the Crouch Position.

4) Emphasize the need to perform the stunt above a well matted area.

5) Stress the importance of using the overhand grip.

6) Make certain the students understand the importance of using firm grips throughout the performance of the stunt.

7) Discuss the need to keep the arms locked throughout the performance of the stunt.

8) Explain the need to position the shoulders above the hands before lifting the legs backward and upward to place them on top of the parallel bars.

9) Tell the students to position the hands on the parallel bars a comfortable distance in front of the lower thighs and knees.

10) Define the term diagonal and relate it to the positioning of the lower legs across the bars.

11) Assist students, if necessary.

SPOTTING HINTS

Position yourself next to the parallel bars while being slightly in front of and to the side of the student. On your signal, instruct the student to perform the Crouch Position. As the student places the hands on the parallel bars in front of and between the legs, grasp the student's near wrist with your front hand and grasp the back of the student's closest upper arm near the armpit with your back hand. The fingers of your back hand circle toward the front of the student's upper arm. Give the student the necessary support with your back hand to be able to maintain balance and stability while lifting the legs backward and upward to place them on top of the parallel bars. If possible, loosen your grips without losing physical contact in order to give the student some independence while performing the stunt; however, be ready to tighten your grips if the student loses balance or begins to fall forward or backward. Make certain you position yourself properly so as not to place undue pressure on your lower back or other potentially weak areas of your body. Do not overspot. Instead, have the student perform the Crouch Position by providing a minimum amount of spotting necessary to allow for a successful and safe performance of the stunt. Continue to give individualized assistance using the preceding method. If possible, encourage the student to practice the Crouch Position without assistance.

V-SEAT

STARTING POSITION
Begin in a Left or Right Side Seat position at the center of the parallel bars.

PERFORMANCE
While keeping the back straight and the head level in a semi-erect position, lift both legs in front of the body. In the process, move the body across the bar so the bar rests against the center part of the side of the outside buttocks. The hands remain in the same positions on the bars. Do not perform the V-Seat by sitting on the bar between the buttocks or on the coccyx bone.

FINISHING POSITION
End in a V-Seat position. The body is in a semi-erect position with the back straight. The head is level with the eyes focused forward. The legs are positioned in front of the body. The legs are together and straight with the toes pointed diagonally upward. The body resembles the letter "V".

IMPORTANT TEACHING SUGGESTIONS

1) Take time in the introductory lesson to discuss the mechanics of the V-Seat and follow-up with a demonstration of the stunt by yourself or by a skilled student. If possible, reinforce the discussion and demonstration with a V-Seat chart and/or a related audiovisual aid.

2) Take time in the introductory lesson to individually assess the proper execution of the stunt and make necessary corrections, if needed.

3) Teach the Left and Right Side Seats (refer to page 84 and 86 respectively for teaching guidelines) as the lead-up stunts to the V-Seat.

4) Emphasize the need to perform the stunt above a well matted area.

5) Have the students perform the stunt at the center of the parallel bars until the stunt has been mastered.

6) Stress the importance of using the overhand grip.

7) Make certain the students understand the importance of using a firm grip throughout the performance of the stunt.

8) Discuss the need to perform the V-Seat with the bar against the center of the side of the outside buttocks instead of having the bar rest between the buttocks or on the coccyx bone.

9) Tell the students to keep the back straight with the head level throughout the performance of the stunt.

10) While keeping the legs straight with the toes pointed, challenge the students to lift the legs to position them as close as possible to the body.

11) Discuss the "polished" look of the V-Seat by sitting in a semi-erect position with the back straight, head level, eyes focused forward, legs straight and positioned close to the body, and the toes pointed diagonally upward.

12) Relate the V-Seat to the letter "V" and discuss the relationship.

13) Assist students, if necessary.

SPOTTING HINTS

Position yourself next to the parallel bars while being slightly behind and to the side of the student. Be on the side where the V-Seat will be performed. Grasp the student's near wrist with your front hand and grasp the back of the student's closest upper arm near the student's arm pit with your back hand. The fingers of your back hand circle toward the front of the student's upper arm. On your signal, instruct the student to perform the V-Seat. Give the student the necessary support with your back hand to be able to maintain balance and stability while moving the body across the bar and lifting the legs forward and upward to place them in the proper V-Seat position. Once the legs are in the V-Seat position, give verbal cues to remind the student to keep the back straight, head level, eyes focused forward, legs together and straight with the toes pointed diagonally upward, and to position the legs as close as possible to the body. If possible, loosen your grips without losing physical contact in order to give the student some independence while performing the stunt; however, be ready to tighten your grips if the student loses balance or begins to fall forward, backward, sideward, or downward.

If the student has difficulty lifting the legs forward and upward to place them in the proper V-Seat position, consider the following spotting modification: Maintain a strong, firm grip with your back hand on the student's upper arm, but release your grip on the student's wrist. Use your front hand to help lift and guide the student's legs to place them in the proper V-Seat position. Make certain you give the necessary lift and support with your back hand on the student's upper arm to help the student keep the back straight while sitting in a semi-erect position. Also, make certain the student moves across the bar so the bar rests against the center of the side of the outside buttocks.

Make certain you position yourself properly in both spotting techniques so as not to place undue pressure on your lower back or other potentially weak areas of your body. Do not overspot. Instead, have the student perform the V-Seat by providing a minimum amount of spotting necessary to allow for a successful and safe perform-ance of the stunt. Continue to give individualized assistance using one of the pre-ceding methods. If possible, encourage the student to practice the V-Seat without assistance.

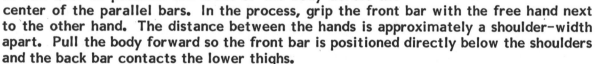

FRONT LEANING REST

STARTING POSITION
Begin in a Left or Right Side Seat position at the center of the parallel bars.

PERFORMANCE
Release the grip of your hand located on the bar (back bar) behind the buttocks; however, maintain the grip of the hand located on the opposite bar (front bar). Begin to roll over to position the front of the body across the center of the parallel bars. In the process, grip the front bar with the free hand next to the other hand. The distance between the hands is approximately a shoulder-width apart. Pull the body forward so the front bar is positioned directly below the shoulders and the back bar contacts the lower thighs.

FINISHING POSITION
End in a Front Leaning Rest position across the center of the parallel bars. The arms are straight with the hands gripping the front bar directly below the shoulders. The hands are a shoulder-width apart. The body is slightly arched and the legs are together and straight with the toes pointed diagonally backward. The lower thighs are posi-tioned on top of the back bar. The head is level with the eyes focused forward.

IMPORTANT TEACHING SUGGESTIONS

1) Take time in the introductory lesson to discuss the mechanics of the Front Lean-ing Rest and follow-up with a demonstration of the stunt by yourself or by a skilled student. If possible, reinforce the discussion and demonstration with a Front Leaning Rest chart and/or a related audiovisual aid.

2) Take time in the introductory lesson to individually assess the proper execution of the stunt and make necessary corrections, if needed.

3) Teach the Left and Right Side Seats (refer to pages 84 and 86 respectively for teaching guidelines) as the lead-up stunts to the Front Leaning Rest.

4)   Emphasize the need to perform the stunt above a well matted area.

5)   Have the students perform the stunt at the center of the parallel bars until the stunt has been mastered.

6)   Stress the importance of using the overhand grip.

7)   Make certain the students understand the importance of using firm grips throughout the performance of the stunt.

8)   Tell the students to roll over slowly and carefully.

9)   Talk about the need to position the hands a shoulder-width apart on the front bar.

10)   Stress the importance of positioning the shoulders directly above the hands to assume the finishing position.

11)   Discuss the "polished" look of the Front Leaning Rest by having the arms straight, shoulders directly above the hands, body slightly arched with the legs together and straight, lower thighs positioned on top of the back bar, toes pointed diagonally backward, head level, and eyes focused forward.

12)   Assist students, if necessary.

SPOTTING HINTS

Position yourself next to the parallel bars while being directly across from the student. The student is performing the Left or Right Side Seat on the opposite bar. Grasp the back of the student's closest upper arm near the student's armpit with your back hand. The fingers of your back hand circle toward the front of the student's upper arm. On your signal, instruct the student to perform the Front Leaning Rest. Give the student the necessary support with your back hand to be able to maintain balance and stability while rolling the body over to position the front of the body across the bars. At the same time, grasp the student's other arm near the student's armpit or within the armpit with your front hand. Give the student the necessary support and lift with your front hand to allow the student to grip the front bar while rolling the body over to place it across the bars. Once the student has rolled over to place the body across the bars, tell the student to pull the body forward to position the shoulders directly above the front bar. When the student has assumed the Front Leaning Rest position, remind the student to straighten the arms while keeping the hands a shoulder-width apart, slightly arch the body with the legs together and straight, point the toes diagonally backward, lift the head to a level position with the eyes focused forward, and make certain the lower thighs are on top of the back bar. If possible, loosen your grips without losing physical contact in order to give the student some independence while performing the stunt, however, be ready to tighten your grips if the student loses balance and begins to fall forward, backward, sideward, or downward. Make certain you position yourself properly so as not to place undue pressure on your lower back or other potentially weak areas of your body. Do not overspot. Instead, have the student perform the Front Leaning Rest by providing a minimum amount of spotting necessary to allow for a successful and safe performance of the stunt. Continue to give individualized assistance using the preceding method. If possible, encourage the student to practice the Front Leaning Rest without assistance.

KNEE SCALE

STARTING POSITION
Begin in a Left or Right Side Seat position at the center of the parallel bars.

PERFORMANCE
Release the grip of the hand located on the bar (back bar) behind the buttocks; however, maintain the grip of the hand located on the opposite bar (front bar). Begin to roll over to position the front of the body across the center of the parallel bars. In the process, grip the front bar with the free hand next to the other hand. The distance between the hands is approximately a shoulder-width apart. Place one knee on the back bar and push-off the knee to assume a two hands and one knee crawling position across the bars with the other leg extended backward.

FINISHING POSITION
End in a Knee Scale position across the center of the parallel bars. The arms are straight with the hands gripping the front bar directly below the shoulders. The hands are a shoulder-width apart. The back is slightly arched and one knee is on top of the back bar with the foot and toes pointed backward. The other leg is straight and extended backward with the toes pointed backward. The head is lifted with the eyes focused forward.

IMPORTANT TEACHING SUGGESTIONS

1) Take time in the introductory lesson to discuss the mechanics of the Knee Scale and follow-up with a demonstration of the stunt by yourself or by a skilled student. If possible, reinforce the discussion and demonstration with a Knee Scale chart and/or a related audiovisual aid.

2) Take time in the introductory lesson to individually assess the proper execution of the stunt and make necessary corrections, if needed.

3) Teach the Left and Right Side Seats (refer to pages 84 and 86 respectively for teaching guidelines) as lead-up stunts to the Knee Scale.

4) Emphasize the need to perform the stunt above a well matted area.

5) Have the students perform the stunt at the center of the parallel bars until the stunt has been mastered.

6) Stress the importance of using the overhand grip.

7) Make certain the students understand the importance of using firm grips throughout the performance of the stunt.

8) Tell the students to roll over slowly and carefully.

9) Talk about the need to position the hands a shoulder-width apart on the front bar.

10) Stress the importance of positioning the shoulders directly above the hands when assuming the finishing position.

11) Tell the students to position the support knee in a comfortable position on top of the back bar.

12) Discuss the "polished" look of the Knee Scale by having the arms straight, shoulders directly above the hands, back slightly arched, one knee on top of the back bar with the foot and toes pointed backward, the other leg straight and extended backward with the toes pointed backward, head lifted, and eyes focused forward.

13) Assist students, if necessary.

SPOTTING HINTS

Position yourself next to the parallel bars while being directly across from the student. The student is performing the Left or Right Side Seat on the opposite bar. Grasp the front of the student's closest upper arm near the student's arm pit with your front hand. The fingers of your front hand circle toward the back of the student's upper arm. On your signal, instruct the student to perform the Knee Scale. Give the student the necessary support and lift with your front hand to be able to maintain balance and stability while rolling the body over to position the front of the body across the bars. Use your back hand to grasp the student's near hip. Give the student the necessary support and lift with your back hand to be able to place the knee on the back bar and push-off the knee to lift the body into the three point crawling position. When the student has assumed the Knee Scale position, remind the student to straighten the arms while keeping the hands a shoulder-width apart, position the shoulders directly above the hands, place a slight arch in the back, maintain the support knee in a comfortable position on the back bar with the foot and toes pointed backward, extend the other leg backward with the toes pointed backward, and keep the head lifted with the eyes focused forward. If possible, loosen your grips without losing physical contact in order to give the student some independence while performing the stunt; however, be ready to tighten your grips if the student loses balance and begins to fall forward, backward, sideward, or downward. Make certain you position yourself properly so as not to place undue pressure on your lower back or other potentially weak areas of your body. Do not overspot. Instead, have the student perform the Knee Scale by providing a minimum amount of spotting necessary to allow for a successful and safe performance of the stunt. Continue to give individualized assistance using the preceding method. If possible, encourage the student to practice the Knee Scale without assistance.

HAND KNEE HANG

STARTING POSITION
Begin in a bent leg and straight back semi-standing position inside the center of the parallel bars with the hands in an overhand grip around the outside of the bars. The arms are bent with the elbows in front of the shoulders and directly below the hands. The elbows are flexed at 90° angles. The head is level with the eyes focused forward.

PERFORMANCE
While maintaining a firm grip, push-off with the feet and pull upward with the arms

to bring the knees toward the chest while lifting the hips. Continue the upward movement to allow the legs, from knees to feet, to pass between and slightly above the bars. Then, stop the upward movement and separate the legs to catch the back of the knees on top of the bars. Allow the legs, from knees to feet, to hang over the sides of the bars.

FINISHING POSITION
End in a Hand Knee Hang position with the legs, from knees to toes, hanging over the sides of the bars. The toes are pointed diagonally sideward. The arms are straight and the hips are forward to create a slight arch in the back. The head is aligned with the body and the eyes are focused backward.

IMPORTANT TEACHING SUGGESTIONS

1) Take time in the introductory lesson to discuss the mechanics of the Hand Knee Hang and follow-up with a demonstration of the stunt by yourself or by a skilled student. If possible, reinforce the discussion and demonstration with a Hand Knee Hang chart and/or a related audiovisual aid.

2) Take time in the introductory lesson to individually assess the proper execution of the stunt and make necessary corrections, if needed.

3) Emphasize the need to perform the stunt over a well matted area.

4) Have the students perform the stunt at the center of the parallel bars until the stunt has been mastered.

5) Stress the importance of using the overhand grip.

6) Make certain the students understand the importance of using a firm grip throughout the performance of the stunt.

7) Explain why it is advantageous to begin the stunt with the arms bent rather than to have the arms straight. By having the arms bent, the shoulders are closer to the bars. This permits more efficient use of the muscles in the arms, shoulders, chest, and upper back to help maneuver the body.

8) Tell the students to lift the legs, from knees to feet, slightly higher than the bars to be able to separate the legs to catch the back of the knees on top of the bars.

9) Discuss the "polished" look of the Hand Knee Hang by having the arms straight, back slightly arched, toes pointed diagonally sideward, and the head properly aligned with the body.

10) Assist students, if necessary.

SPOTTING HINTS

Position yourself next to the parallel bars while being beside the student at his/her level. Depending on your height, and the height of the parallel bars, you will be positioned in a kneeling, squatting, or bent leg straddle position. Grasp the student's closest wrist with your back hand. On your signal, instruct the student to perform the Hand Knee Hang. Use your front hand to assist the upward movement of the legs and feet. Usually, assistance can be given by placing your front hand behind the student's closest knee to give additional lift and power to the upward movement. Remove your hand as soon as the student's legs, from knees to feet, pass slightly above and between the bars so the student can separate the legs to allow them to hang over the sides of the bars. Make certain your grip on the wrist is a firm one in case the student's hand slips off the bar. If so, give a gentle but forceful lift to stop the student from falling to the mat.

Make certain you position yourself properly so as not to place undue pressure on your lower back or other potentially weak areas of your body. Do not overspot. Instead, have the student perform the Hand Knee Hang by providing a minimum amount of spotting necessary to allow for a successful and safe performance of the stunt. Continue to give individualized assistance using the preceding method. If possible, encourage the student to practice the Hand Knee Hang without assistance.

SKIN THE CAT

STARTING POSITION
Begin in a bent leg and straight back semi-standing position inside the center of the parallel bars with the hands in an overhand grip around the outside of the bars. The arms are bent with the elbows in front of the shoulders and directly below the hands. The elbows are flexed at 90° angles. The head is level with the eyes focused forward.

PERFORMANCE
While maintaining a firm grip, push-off with the feet and pull upward with the arms to bring the knees to the chest while lifting the hips to begin the backward rotation. At the same time, tuck the chin to the chest. Continue the backward rotation so the body begins to pass between the straightened arms in a tight, tuck position. After the body passes between the arms, start to open the body to allow the legs to move downward so the balls of the feet contact the mat. Untuck the chin to place the head in a position to be able to focus the eyes on the mat and feet. To complete the stunt, push-off with the balls of the feet to lift the hips and bring the knees to the chest to begin the forward rotation. At the same time, tuck the chin to the chest. Continue the forward rotation so the body begins to pass between the straightened arms in a tight, tuck position. After the body passes between the arms, start to open the body to allow the legs to move downward so the feet contact the mat. Untuck the chin to place the head in a position to be able to focus the eyes forward.

FINISHING POSITION
End in a bent leg and straight back semi-standing position inside the center of the parallel bars with the hands in an overhead grip around the outside of the bars. The arms are bent with the elbows in front of the shoulders and directly below the hands.

The elbows are flexed at 90° angles. The head is level with the eyes focused forward.

IMPORTANT TEACHING SUGGESTIONS

1) Take time in the introductory lesson to discuss the mechanics of the Skin The Cat and follow-up with a demonstration of the stunt by yourself or by a skilled student. If possible, reinforce the discussion and demonstration with a Skin The Cat chart and/or a related audiovisual aid.

2) Take time in the introductory lesson to individually assess the proper execution of the stunt and make necessary corrections, if needed.

3) Emphasize the need to perform the stunt above a well matted area.

4) Have the students perform the stunt at the center of the parallel bars until the stunt has been mastered.

5) Stress the importance of using the overhand grip.

6) Make certain the students understand the importance of using a firm grip throughout the performance of the stunt.

7) Explain why it is advantageous to begin the stunt with the arms bent rather than to have the arms straight. By having the arms bent, the shoulders are closer to the bars. This permits more efficient use of the muscles in the arms, shoulders, chest, and upper back to help maneuver the body.

8) Tell the students to perform the backward and forward rotations in tight, tuck positions.

9) Stress the need to push-off with the feet to begin the forward rotation to return to the finishing position.

10) Encourage the students to complete the forward rotation by allowing the feet to return to the mat in a safe, controlled manner.

11) Assist students, if necessary.

SPOTTING HINTS

Position yourself next to the parallel bars while being beside the student at his/her level. Depending on your height, and the height of the parallel bars, you will be positioned in a kneeling, squatting, or bent leg straddle position. For the backward rotation of the stunt, grasp the student's closest wrist with your back hand. On your signal, instruct the student to perform the backward rotation of the Skin The Cat. Use your front hand to assist the backward rotation. Usually, assistance can be given by placing your front hand behind the student's closest knee to give additional lift and power to the backward rotation. Remove your hand as soon as the student begins to tuck and pass between the straightened arms. Make certain your grip on the student's wrist is a firm one in case the student's hand slips off the bar. If so, give a gentle but forceful lift to stop the student from falling to the mat.

After the student has completed the backward rotation and his/her feet are on the mat, change your grip hand. Use your front hand to grasp the student's closest wrist. On your signal, instruct the student to perform the forward rotation of the Skin The Cat. Use your back hand to assist the forward rotation. Usually, assistance can be given by placing your back hand under the student's closest hip to give additional lift and power to the forward rotation. Remove your hand as soon as the student begins to tuck and pass between the straightened arms. Once again, make certain your grip on the wrist is a firm one in case the student's hand slips off the bar. If so, give a gentle but forceful lift to stop the student from falling to the mat.

Make certain you position yourself properly so as not to place undue pressure on your lower back or other potentially weak areas of your body. <u>Do not</u> overspot. Instead, have the student perform the Skin The Cat by providing a minimum amount of spotting necessary to allow for a successful and safe performance of the stunt. Continue to give individualized assistance using the preceding method. If possible, encourage the student to practice the Skin The Cat without assistance.

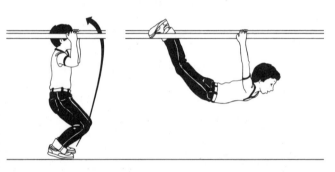

BIRD'S NEST

STARTING POSITION
Begin in a bent leg and straight back semi-standing position inside the center of the parallel bars with the hands in an overhand grip around the outside of the bars. The arms are bent with the elbows in front of the shoulders and directly below the hands. The elbows are flexed at 90° angles. The head is level with the eyes focused forward.

PERFORMANCE
While maintaining a firm grip, push-off with the feet and pull upward with the arms to bring the knees to the chest while lifting the hips to begin the backward movement. At the same time, tuck the chin to the chest. Continue the backward movement so the body begins to pass between the straightened arms in a semi-tuck position. Then, start to open the body and place the insteps of the feet on top of the inside of the bars. The midsection of the body continues it's backward and downward movement while the feet slide backward on the bars. The head becomes lifted.

FINISHING POSITION
End in an inverted, arch position with the hands in an overhand grip on the outside of the bars. The insteps of the feet are on top of the inside of the bars. The arms are straight and the head is lifted with eyes focused forward.

IMPORTANT TEACHING SUGGESTIONS

1) Take time in the introductory lesson to discuss the mechanics of the Bird's Nest and follow-up with a demonstration of the stunt by yourself or a skilled student. If possible, reinforce the discussion and demonstration with a Bird's Nest chart and/or a related audiovisual aid.

2) Take time in the introductory lesson to individually assess the proper execution of the stunt and make necessary corrections, if needed.

3) Emphasize the need to perform the stunt above a well matted area.

4) Make certain the students perform the Bird's Nest in the center or toward the front of the parallel bars. There has to be enough distance on the parallel bars behind the student to allow for safe and proper placement of the insteps of the feet on top of the inside of the bars. Be careful that the student's feet do not slide off the ends of the parallel bars.

5) Stress the importance of using the overhand grip.

6) Make certain the students understand the importance of using a firm grip throughout the performance of the stunt.

7) Explain why it is advantageous to begin the stunt with the arms bent rather than to have the arms straight. By having the arms bent, the shoulders are closer to the bars. This permits more efficient use of the muscles in the arms, shoulders, chest, and upper back to help maneuver the body.

8) Tell the students to gently place the insteps of the feet on top of the inside of the bars and have them slide the feet a comfortable distance away from the hands.

9) Have the students lower their hips as the feet slide backward on top of the inside of the bars away from the hands. By having the hips drop, it places an arch in the back.

10) Explain the need to lift the chin to allow the eyes to be focused forward instead of keeping the chin tucked to the chest.

11) Assist students, if necessary.

SPOTTING HINTS

Position yourself next to the parallel bars while being beside the student at his/her level. Depending on your height and the height of the parallel bars, you will be positioned in a kneeling, squatting, or bent leg straddle position. Grasp the student's closest wrist with your back hand. On your signal, instruct the student to perform the Bird's Nest. Use your front hand to assist the upward and backward movements. Usually, assistance can be given by placing your front hand behind the student's closest knee to give additional lift and power to the upward and backward movements. Remove your hand as soon as the student begins to tuck and position his/her body between the straightened arms. Then, change your grip hand to give your back hand the opportunity to grasp the student's near ankle to help the student place the near instep on top of the inside of the closest bar. When complete, grab the other ankle to help place the far instep on top of the inside of the other bar, if necessary. Lastly, use your back hand to help the student lower the hips to attain the proper inverted, arch position. During the grip exchange, be sure that one of your grips is maintained at all times. Make certain your grip on the wrist is a firm one, regardless of your grip hand, in case the student's hand slips off the bar. If so, give a gentle but forceful lift to stop the student from falling to the mat.

Make certain you position yourself properly so as not to place undue pressure on your lower back or other potentially weak areas of your body. Do not overspot. Instead, have the student perform the Bird's Nest by providing a minimum amount of spotting necessary to allow for a successful and safe performance of the stunt. Continue to give individualized assistance using the preceding method. If possible, encourage the student to practice the Bird's Nest without assistance.

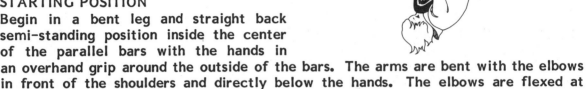

TUCK HANG

STARTING POSITION
Begin in a bent leg and straight back semi-standing position inside the center of the parallel bars with the hands in an overhand grip around the outside of the bars. The arms are bent with the elbows in front of the shoulders and directly below the hands. The elbows are flexed at 90° angles. The head is level with the eyes focused forward.

PERFORMANCE
While maintaining a firm grip, push-off with the feet and pull upward with the arms to bring the knees to the chest while lifting the hips. At the same time, tuck the chin to the chest. Continue the movement until the body begins to pass between the straightened arms in a tight, tuck position.

FINISHING POSITION
End in an inverted, balanced, Tuck Hang position between the straightened arms. The knees and chin are tucked to the chest and the heels are close to the buttocks.

IMPORTANT TEACHING SUGGESTIONS

1) Take time in the introductory lesson to discuss the mechanics of the Tuck Hang and follow-up with a demonstration of the stunt by yourself or by a skilled student. If possible, reinforce the discussion and demonstration with a Tuck Hang chart and/or related audiovisual aid.

2) Take time in the introductory lesson to individually assess the proper execution of the stunt and make necessary corrections, if needed.

3) Teach the Hand Knee Hang (refer to pages 100 and 101 for teaching guidelines) as the lead-up stunt to the Tuck Hang.

4) <u>Do not</u> permit a student to attempt a Tuck Hang until the student has success- fully mastered the Hand Knee Hang.

5) Emphasize the need to perform the stunt above a well matted area.

6) Have the student perform the stunt at the center of the parallel bars until the stunt has been mastered.

7) Stress the importance of using the overhand grip.

8) Make certain the students understand the importance of using a firm grip throughout the performance of the stunt.

9) Explain why it is advantageous to begin the stunt with the arms bent rather

than to have the arms straight. By having the arms bent, the shoulders are closer to the bars. This permits more efficient use of the muscles in the arms, shoulders, chest, and upper back to help maneuver the body.

10) Tell the students to stop the backward movement as soon as the tucked body is positioned between the straightened arms.

11) Discuss the word "balance" and the role it plays in helping to keep the body in an inverted, tight, Tuck Hang position between the straightened arms.

12) Discuss the "polished" look of the Tuck Hang by being in an inverted, balanced, tight tuck position between straightened arms with the knees and chin tucked to the chest and the heels close to the buttocks.

13) Assist students, if necessary.

SPOTTING HINTS

Position yourself next to the parallel bars while being beside the student at his/her level. Depending on your height, and the height of the parallel bars, you will be positioned in a kneeling, squatting, or bent leg straddle position. Grasp the student's closest wrist with your back hand. On your signal, instruct the student to perform the Tuck Hang. Use your front hand to assist the upward and backward movements. Usually, assistance can be given by placing your front hand behind the student's closest knee to give additional lift and power to the upward and backward movements. Remove your hand as soon as the student begins to tuck and position his/her body between the straightened arms. If necessary, change your grip hand to allow your back hand the opportunity to grasp the student's near ankle to help the student maintain the inverted, balanced, Tuck Hang position. During the grip exchange, be sure the one grip is maintained at all times. Make certain your grip on the student's wrist is a firm one, regardless of your grip hand, in case the student's hand slips off the bar. If so, give a gentle but forceful lift to stop the student from falling to the mat.

Make certain you position yourself properly so as not to place undue pressure on your lower back or other potentially weak areas of your body. <u>Do not</u> overspot. Instead, have the student perform the Tuck Hang by providing a minimum amount of spotting necessary to allow for a successful and safe performance of the stunt. Continue to give individualized assistance using the preceding method. If possible, encourage the student to practice the Tuck Hang without assistance.

PIKE HANG

STARTING POSITION
Begin in a bent leg and straight back semi-standing position inside the center of the parallel bars with the hands in an overhand grip around the outside of the bars. The arms are bent with the elbows in front of the shoulders and directly below the hands. The elbows are flexed at 90° angles. The head is level with the eyes focused forward.

PERFORMANCE
While maintaining a firm grip, push-off with the feet and pull upward with the arms

to bring the knees close to the chest while lifting the hips. At the same time, position the chin close to the chest. Continue the movement until the semi-tucked body begins to pass between the straightened arms. At this time, extend the legs to place them in front of the hips with the toes pointed backward.

FINISHING POSITION
End in an inverted, balanced, Pike Hang position between the straightened arms. The legs are straight with the toes pointed backward. The chin is close to the chest with the eyes focused on the knees.

IMPORTANT TEACHING SUGGESTIONS

1) Take time in the introductory lesson to discuss the mechanics of the Pike Hang and follow-up with a demonstration of the stunt by yourself or by a skilled student. If possible, reinforce the discussion and demonstration with a Pike Hang chart and/or a related audiovisual aid.

2) Take time in the introductory lesson to individually assess the proper execution of the stunt and make necessary corrections, if necessary.

3) Teach the Tuck Hang (refer to page 106 for teaching guidelines) as the lead-up stunt to the Pike Hang.

4) Emphasize the need to perform the stunt above a well matted area.

5) Have the student perform the stunt at the center of the parallel bars until the stunt has been mastered.

6) Stress the importance of using the overhand grip.

7) Make certain the students understand the importance of using a firm grip throughout the performance of the stunt.

8) Explain why it is advantageous to begin the stunt with the arms bent rather than to have the arms straight. By having the arms bent, the shoulders are closer to the bars. This permits more efficient use of the muscles in the arms, shoulders, chest, and upper back to help maneuver the body.

9) Tell the students to stop the backward movement as soon as the semi-tucked body is positioned between the straightened arms.

10) Discuss the word "balance" and the role it plays in helping to keep the body in an inverted, Pike Hang position between the straightened arms.

11) Discuss the "polished" look of the Pike Hang by having the legs together and straight with the toes pointed backward and the chin close to the chest with the eyes focused on the knees.

12) Assist the students, if necessary.

SPOTTING HINTS

Position yourself next to the parallel bars while being beside the student at his/her level. Depending on your height, and the height of the parallel bars, you will be positioned in a kneeling, squatting, or bent leg straddle position. Grasp the student's closest wrist with your back hand. On your signal, instruct the student to perform the Pike Hang. Use your front hand to assist the upward and backward movements. Usually, assistance can be given by placing your front hand behind the student's closest knee to give additional lift and power to the upward and backward movements. Remove your hand as soon as the student's semi-tucked body begins to be positioned between the student's straightened arms. If necessary, change your grip hand to allow your back hand the opportunity to grasp the student's near ankle to help the student maintain the inverted, balanced, Pike Hang position. During the grip exchange, be sure that one grip is maintained at all times. Make certain your grip on the student's wrist is a firm one, regardless of which grip hand you use, in case the student's hand slips off the bar. If so, give a gentle but forceful lift to stop the student from falling to the mat.

Make certain you position yourself properly so as not to place undue pressure on your lower back or other potentially weak areas of your body. <u>Do not</u> overspot. Instead, have the student perform the Pike Hang by providing a minimum amount of spotting necessary to allow for a successful and safe performance of the stunt. Continue to give individualized assistance using the preceding method. If possible, encourage the student to practice the Pike Hang without assistance.

INVERTED HANG

STARTING POSITION
Begin in a bent leg and straight back semi-standing position inside the center of the parallel bars with the hands in an overhand grip around the outside of the bars. The arms are bent with the elbows in front of the shoulders and directly below the hands. The elbows are flexed at 90° angles. The head is level with the eyes focused forward.

PERFORMANCE
While maintaining a firm grip, push-off with the feet and pull upward with the arms to bring the knees close to the chest while lifting the hips. At the same time, position the chin close to the chest. Continue the movement until the semi-tucked body begins to pass between the straightened arms. At this time, start to open the body to extend the legs and feet upward while straightening the back and untucking the chin.

FINISHING POSITION
End in a balanced, Inverted Hang position between the straightened arms. The body is straight from shoulders to pointed toes. The head is tilted backward with the eyes focused downward.

IMPORTANT TEACHING SUGGESTIONS

1) Take time in the introductory lesson to discuss the mechanics of the Inverted Hang and follow-up with a demonstration of the stunt by yourself or by a skilled student. If possible, reinforce the discussion and demonstration with an Inverted Hang chart and/or a related audiovisual aid.

2) Take time in the introductory lesson to individually assess the proper execution of the stunt and make necessary corrections, if necessary.

3) Teach the Tuck Hang (refer to page 106 for teaching guidelines) as the lead-up stunt to the Inverted Hang.

4) Emphasize the need to perform the stunt above a well matted area.

5) Have the student perform the stunt at the center of the parallel bars until the stunt has been mastered.

6) Stress the importance of using the overhand grip.

7) Make certain the students understand the importance of using a firm grip throughout the performance of the stunt.

8) Explain why it is advantageous to begin the stunt with the arms bent rather than to have the arms straight. By having the arms bent, the shoulders are closer to the bars. This permits more efficient use of the muscles in the arms, shoulders, chest, and upper back to help maneuver the body.

9) Tell the students to stop the backward movement as soon as the semi-tucked body is positioned between the straightened arms.

10) Discuss the word "balance" and the role it plays in helping to keep the body in an Inverted Hang position between the straightened arms.

11) Tell the students to slowly open the body from the semi-tuck position to assume the proper Inverted Hang position. Balance is easier to maintain if the movements are slow and controlled.

12) Discuss the "polished" look of the Inverted Hang by having the body straight from shoulders to pointed toes with the head tilted backward and the eyes focused downward.

13) Assist students, if necessary.

SPOTTING HINTS

Position yourself next to the parallel bars while being beside the student at his/her level. Depending on your height, and the height of the parallel bars, you will be positioned in a kneeling, squatting, or bent leg straddle position. Grasp the student's closest wrist with your back hand. On your signal, instruct the student to perform the Inverted Hang. Use your front hand to assist the upward and backward movements. Usually, assistance can be given by placing your front hand behind the student's closest knee to give additional lift and power to the student's upward and backward movements. Slide your hand forward toward the student's closest ankle as soon as the student begins to position his/her semi-tucked body between the straightened arms. Next, reposition your front hand above the nearest bar to grasp the student's closest ankle to help the student attain and then maintain the balanced, Inverted Hang position. Make certain your grip on the student's wrist is a firm one in case the student's hand slips off the bar. If so, give a gentle but forceful lift to stop the student from falling to the mat.

Make certain you position yourself properly so as not to place undue pressure on your lower back or other potentially weak areas of your body. <u>Do not</u> overspot. Instead, have the student perform the Inverted Hang by providing a minimum amount of spotting necessary to allow for a successful and safe performance of the stunt. Continue to give individualized assistance using the preceding method. If possible, encourage the student to practice the Inverted Hang without assistance.

Chapter – 6

TURNS

INTRODUCTION

The Turns Chapter includes a detailed explanation of three parallel bars turns. Each explanation includes three phases: Starting Position, Performance, and Finishing Position. In addition, each parallel bars turn has a list of Important Teaching Suggestions and a Spotting Hints section.

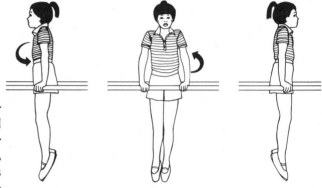

STRAIGHT ARM SUPPORT TURN

STARTING POSITION
Begin in a Straight Arm Support position at the center of the parallel bars. The arms are straight and positioned along the sides of the body. The head is level and the body is straight up and down with the shoulders positioned directly above the hands. The toes are pointed downward.

PERFORMANCE
While keeping the arms straight, head level, and the body straight up and down with the toes pointed downward, perform a one quarter turn to the left. In the process, take the right hand off the far bar and grip the near bar beside the right hip. At the same time, position the hips against the inside of the near bar. By making the one quarter turn to the left, the body is facing away from the parallel bars in a Straight Arm Support position against the inside of the near bar. Continue to turn to the left to perform another one quarter turn by taking the left hand off the near bar and reaching back to grip the far bar beside the left hip.

FINISHING POSITION
End in a Straight Arm Support position at the center of the parallel bars. The arms are straight and positioned along the sides of the body. The head is level and the body is straight up and down with the shoulders positioned directly above the hands. The toes are pointed downward.

IMPORTANT TEACHING SUGGESTIONS

1) Take time in the introductory lesson to discuss the mechanics of the Straight Arm Support Turn and follow-up with a demonstration of the turn by yourself or by a skilled student. If possible, reinforce the discussion and demonstration with a Straight Arm Support Turn chart and/or a related audiovisual aid.

2) Take time in the introductory lesson to individually assess the proper execution of the turn and make necessary corrections, if needed.

3) Teach the Straight Arm Support (refer to page 78 for teaching guidelines) as the lead-up stunt to the Straight Arm Support Turn.

4) <u>Do not</u> permit a student to attempt the Straight Arm Support Turn until the student has successfully mastered the Straight Arm Support.

5) Emphasize the need to perform the turn above a well matted area.

6) Have the student perform the turn at the center of the parallel bars until the turn has been mastered.

7) Stress the importance of using the overhand grip.

8) Make certain the students understand the importance of using firm grips throughout the performance of the turn.

9) Explain how the body performs the complete one half turn while making grip changes.

10) Discuss the term "balance" and the role it plays after the completion of the first one quarter turn when the body is facing away from the parallel bars in a Straight Arm Support position against the inside of the near bar.

11) Tell the students to make quick but controlled one quarter turns to grip the opposite bar.

12) Tell the students to push downward with the hand that will leave one bar to grip the opposite bar prior to making the move. The downward push will give the body additional height with corresponding additional time to make the one quarter turn.

13) Tell the students, who lack sufficient upper body strength to be able to perform the Straight Arm Support position against the inside of the near bar, to compensate by bending slightly at the waist and placing the upper body above and slightly in front of the bar. By modifying the Straight Arm Support position in this way, the students will be able to hold the position without having to lower the feet to the mat.

14) Encourage the students to perform the complete one half turn cautiously and under complete control.

15) Assist students, if necessary.

SPOTTING HINTS

Position yourself next to the parallel bars while being directly beside the student. Grasp the outside of the student's closest upper arm with your front hand so your fingers wrap around the inside of the student's arm. Reach across the student's chest with your back hand to place your hand under the student's far under arm so your fingers grip the student's upper back and your thumb grips the student's upper chest areas. On your signal, instruct the student to perform the Straight Arm Support Turn. As the student performs the first one quarter turn, help steady and support the student's movements by using firm grips. Reposition your grips slightly to compensate for the first one quarter turn then maintain your firm grips while the student performs the second quarter turn. Be ready to give a forceful but gentle lift if the student loses his/her balance or begins to fall to the mat. If possible, loosen your grips without losing physical contact in order to give the student some independence while performing the turn; however, be ready to tighten your grips if the student loses balance or is unable to grip the opposite bar during the turns and starts to fall to the mat. Make certain you position yourself properly so as not to place undue pressure on your lower back or other potentially weak areas of your body. <u>Do not</u> overspot. Instead, have the student perform the Straight Arm Support Turn by providing a minimum amount of spotting necessary to allow for a successful and safe performance of the turn. Continue to give individualized assistance using the preceding method. If possible, encourage the student to practice the Straight Arm Support Turn without assistance.

VARIATION

Have the student perform a Straight Arm Support Turn by turning to the right instead of the left.

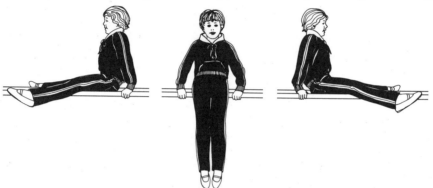

STRADDLE SEAT TURN

STARTING POSITION
Begin in a Straddle Seat position at the center of the parallel bars. The legs are straight with the toes pointed diagonally sideward. The back is straight and the head is level with the eyes focused forward. The hands are gripping the bars beside the buttocks.

PERFORMANCE
While keeping the back straight, the head level, and the eyes focused forward, perform a one quarter turn to the left. In the process, swing the right leg across the near bar. Also, take the right hand off the far bar to grip the near bar beside the right buttocks. Then, lower and straighten the right leg to place it beside the left leg with both feet pointed downward. By making the one quarter turn to the left, the body is facing away from the parallel bars while sitting on the edge of the near bar. Continue to turn to the left to perform another one quarter turn by swinging the left leg across the far bar. At the same time, take the left hand off the near bar to grip the far bar beside the left buttocks.

FINISHING POSITION
End in a Straddle Seat position. The legs are straight with the toes pointed diagonally sideward. The back is straight and the head is level with the eyes focused forward. The hands are gripping the bars beside the buttocks.

IMPORTANT TEACHING SUGGESTIONS

1) Take time in the introductory lesson to discuss the mechanics of the Straddle Seat Turn and follow-up with a demonstration of the turn by yourself or by a skilled student. If possible, reinforce the discussion and demonstration with a Straddle Seat Turn chart and/or a related audiovisual aid.

2) Take time in the introductory lesson to individually assess the proper execution of the turn and make necessary corrections, if needed.

3) Teach the Straddle Seat (refer to page 83 for teaching guidelines) as the lead-up stunt to the Straddle Seat Turn.

4) Emphasize the need to perform the turn above a well matted area.

5) Have the student perform the turn at the center of the parallel bars until the turn has been mastered.

6) Stress the importance of using the overhand grip.

7) Make certain the students understand the importance of using firm grips throughout the performance of the turn.

8) Explain how the body performs the complete one half turn while making grip changes.

9) Discuss the term "balance" and the role it plays after the completion of the first one quarter turn when the body is facing away from the parallel bars while sitting on the outside edge of the near bar.

10) Encourage the students to perform the complete one half turn cautiously and under complete control.

11) Assist students, if necessary.

SPOTTING HINTS

Position yourself next to the parallel bars while being directly beside the student. Grasp the outside of the student's closest upper arm with your front hand so your fingers wrap around the inside of the student's arm. Reach across the student's chest with your back hand to place your hand under the student's far under arm so your fingers grip the student's upper back and your thumb grips the student's upper chest areas. On your signal, instruct the student to perform the Straddle Seat Turn. As the student performs the first one quarter turn, help steady the student's movements by using firm grips. Reposition your grips slightly to compensate for the first one quarter turn then maintain the same firm grips while the student performs the second quarter turn. Be ready to give a forceful but gentle lift if the student loses his/her balance and begins to slip off the bar. If possible, loosen your grips without losing physical contact in order to give the student some independence while performing the turn; however, be ready to tighten your grips if the student loses balance and begins to fall forward, backward, or sideward. Make certain you position yourself properly so as not to place undue pressure on your lower back or other potentially weak areas of your body. Do not overspot. Instead, have the student perform the Straddle Seat Turn by providing a minimum amount of spotting necessary to allow for a successful and safe performance of the turn. Continue to give individualized assistance using the preceding method. If possible, encourage the student to practice the Straddle Seat Turn without assistance.

VARIATION

Have the student perform a Straddle Seat Turn by turning to the right instead of the left.

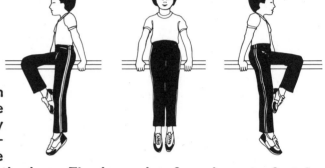

SIDE SEAT TURN

STARTING POSITION
Begin in a Left Side Seat position on the near bar at the center of the parallel bars. The left leg is vertically straight with the toes pointed downward. The right leg is bent with the upper leg from hip to knee sitting on the bar. The lower leg from knee to foot is angled toward the left knee with the right foot on top of the left knee. The back is straight and the head is level with the eyes focused forward. The left hand is gripping the bar behind the left buttocks and the right hand is gripping the far bar directly across from the right side of the body.

PERFORMANCE
While keeping the back straight, the head level, and the eyes focused forward, perform a one quarter turn to the left. In the process, take the right hand off the far bar to grip the near bar beside the right buttocks. At the same time, straighten the right leg and place it beside the left leg with both feet pointed downward. By making the one quarter turn to the left, the body is facing away from the parallel bars while sitting on the edge of the near bar. Continue to turn to the left to perform another one quarter turn.

FINISHING POSITION
End in a Right Side Seat position on the near bar. The right leg is vertically straight with the toes pointed downward. The left leg is bent with the upper leg from hip to knee sitting on the bar. The lower leg from knee to foot is angled toward the right knee with the left foot on top of the right knee. The back is straight and the head is level with the eyes focused forward. The right hand is gripping the bar behind the right buttocks and the left hand is gripping the far bar directly across from the left side of the body.

IMPORTANT TEACHING SUGGESTIONS

1) Take time in the introductory lesson to discuss the mechanics of the Side Seat Turn and follow-up with a demonstration of the turn by yourself or by a skilled student. If possible, reinforce the discussion and demonstration with a Side Seat Turn chart and/or a related audiovisual aid.

2) Take time in the introductory lesson to individually assess the proper execution of the turn and make necessary corrections, if needed.

3) Teach the Left Side Seat and the Right Side Seat (refer to pages 84 and 86 respectively for teaching guidelines) as the lead-up stunts to the Side Seat Turn.

4) Emphasize the need to perform the turn above a well matted area.

5) Have the students perform the turn at the center of the parallel bars until the turn has been mastered.

6) Stress the importance of using the overhand grip.

7) Make certain the students understand the importance of using firm grips throughout the performance of the turn.

8) Explain how the body performs the complete one half turn while making grip changes.

9) Discuss the term "balance" and the role it plays after the completion of the first one quarter turn when the body is facing away from the parallel bars while sitting on the outside edge of the near bar.

10) Encourage the students to perform the complete one half turn cautiously and under complete control.

11) Assist students, if necessary.

SPOTTING HINTS

Position yourself next to the parallel bars while being directly beside the student. Grasp the outside of the student's closest upper arm with your front hand so your fingers wrap around the inside of the student's arm. Reach across the student's chest with your back hand to place your hand under the student's far under arm so your fingers grip the student's upper back and your thumb grips the upper chest areas. On your signal, instruct the student to perform the Side Seat Turn. As the student performs the first one quarter turn, help steady the student's movements by using firm grips. Reposition your grips slightly to compensate for the first one quarter turn then maintain the same firm grips while the student performs the second quarter turn. Be ready to give a forceful but gentle lift if the student loses his/her balance and begins to slip off the bar. If possible, loosen your grips without losing physical contact in order to give the student some independence while performing the turn; however, be ready to tighten your grips if the student loses balance and begins to fall forward, backward, or sideward. Make certain you position yourself properly so as not to place undue pressure on your lower back or other potentially weak areas of your body. Do not overspot. Instead, have the student perform the Side Seat Turn by providing a minimum amount of spotting necessary to allow for a successful and safe performance of the turn. Continue to give individualized assistance using the preceding method. If possible, encourage the student to practice the Side Seat Turn without assistance.

VARIATION

Have the students start in a Right Side Seat position and finish in a Left Side Seat position.

Chapter - 7

DISMOUNTS

INTRODUCTION

The Dismounts Chapter includes a detailed explanation of five parallel bars dismounts. Each explanation includes three phases: Starting Position, Performance, and Finishing Position. In addition, each parallel bars dismount has a list of Important Teaching Suggestions and a Spotting Hints section.

FRONT DISMOUNT

STARTING POSITION
Begin in a Straight Arm Support position at the center of the parallel bars. The arms are straight and positioned along the sides of the body. The head is level and the body is straight up and down with the shoulders positioned directly above the hands. The toes are pointed downward.

PERFORMANCE
While maintaining a firm grip, lift the legs and feet forward and upward to assume a pike position. Then, swing the legs and feet downward, backward and upward into an arch position. Throughout this entire process, keep the arms locked and the shoulders positioned directly above the hands. Make the shoulders the fulcrum of the swing. At the height of the backward swing, with the hips and legs above the bars, push down on the far bar with the far hand and swing the body over the near bar. The front of the body passes above the bar. After the body passes over the bar, lower the legs and feet and land in an upright position on the balls of the feet with the knees bent and the outside arm extended sideward at shoulder level. The weight is balanced above the balls of the feet. At the same time, grasp the near bar with the far hand as the inside hand releases its grip.

FINISHING POSITION
End in a standing position by straightening the legs and lowering the heels to the mat. At the same time, lower the outside arm to place the arm at the side of the body. Also, release the grip of the far hand on the near bar and place the far arm at the side of the body. The body is straight up and down with the head level and the eyes focused forward.

IMPORTANT TEACHING SUGGESTIONS

1) Take time in the introductory lesson to discuss the mechanics of the Front Dismount and follow-up with a demonstration of the dismount by yourself or by a skilled student. If possible, reinforce the discussion and demonstration with a Front Dismount chart and/or a related audiovisual aid.

2) Take time in the introductory lesson to individually assess the proper execution of the dismount and make necessary corrections, if needed.

3) Teach the Straight Arm Support (refer to page 78 for teaching guidelines) and the Swing (refer to page 81 for teaching guidelines) as lead-up stunts to the Front Dismount.

4) Emphasize the need to perform the dismount over a well matted area.

5) Stress the importance of using the overhand grip.

6) Make certain the students understand the importance of using firm grips throughout the performance of the dismount.

7) Stress the need to keep the arms locked and the shoulders directly above the hands throughout the performance of the forward and backward swings.

8) Discuss the term "fulcrum" and relate it to the position of the shoulders throughout the performance of the forward and backward swings.

9) Tell the students to bend at the waist as the legs swing forward and upward to assume the pike position.

10) Discuss the term "balance" and relate it to the equal swinging motion of the legs and feet in front of and in back of the body.

11) Tell the students to keep the toes pointed throughout the forward and backward swings.

12) Stress the need to swing the legs and hips backward and upward above the bars to be able to swing the body over the near bar.

13) Make certain the students swing the body over the near bar at the height of the backward swing.

14) Emphasize the need to push down with a lot of force on the far bar with the far hand to help the body pass over the near bar.

15) Discuss the transfer of grips made with the far hand going from the far bar to the near bar.

16) Tell the students to keep the legs together throughout the entire performance of the Front Dismount.

17) Stress the need to swing the body over the near bar and not allow it to come down on top of the bar.

18) Emphasize proper landing technique: Land in an upright balanced position on the balls of the feet with the knees bent and the head level.

19) Talk about the need to land in a balanced, upright position with the weight centered above the balls of the feet.

20) Encourage the students to land with the outside arm extended sideward at shoulder level, then lower the arm to the side of the body to assume the proper finishing position.

21) Tell the students to use the far hand to create a steady landing during the time the hand grips the near bar.

22) Tell the students to release the grip of the far hand on the near bar only after balance is maintained upon landing.

23) Discuss the "polished" look of the finishing position by having the body straight up and down, heels on the mat, arms at the sides of the body, head level, and the eyes focused forward.

24) Assist students, if needed.

SPOTTING HINTS

Position yourself next to the parallel bars while being slightly behind and to the side of the student. Be on the opposite side where the dismount will be performed. Grasp the student's closest upper arm near the student's arm pit with your front hand. The fingers of your front hand circle toward the back of the student's upper arm. On your signal, instruct the student to perform the Front Dismount. Give the student the necessary support with your front hand to be able to maintain balance and stability while swinging the legs and feet forward and backward. When the student is close to reaching the highest point of the backward swing, grasp the student's closest knee with your back hand by having your fingers circle toward the back of the student's knee with your thumb crossing the front of the student's knee. Help the student swing the legs and feet high enough on the backswing to safely swing the legs and hips above the bars. Assuming the student's backward swing is under control, and the legs and hips are higher than the bars, maintain a firm grip on the student's closest knee with your back hand and push the student's legs and body over the opposite bar. Release your grip on the student's closest knee after the student's body passes over the opposite bar. Maintain your grip on the student's closest upper arm with your front hand throughout the process of the student changing grips from one bar to the other. Release your grip on the student's upper arm after the student has successfully and safely landed using the proper landing technique.

If the student is unable to swing the legs and hips higher than the bars on the backward swing or if the student is unable to keep the body in the proper position throughout the forward and backward swings, do not force the student to perform the Front Dismount. Instead, encourage the student to practice the Swing to be able to maintain balance and stability during the swinging movements while trying to reach a height higher than the bars on the backward swing. When the student achieves success on the backward swing, while maintaining the proper position throughout the forward and backward swings, give the student another opportunity to perform the Front Dismount while being spotted.

Make certain you position yourself properly so as not to place undue pressure on your lower back or other potentially weak areas of your body. Do not overspot. Instead, have the student perform the Front Dismount by providing a minimum amount of spotting necessary for a successful and safe performance of the dismount. Continue to give individualized assistance using the preceding method. If possible, encourage the student to practice the Front Dismount without assistance.

REAR DISMOUNT

STARTING POSITION
Begin in a Straight Arm Support position at the center of the parallel bars. The arms are straight and positioned along the sides of the body. The head is level and the body is straight up and down with the shoulders positioned directly above the hands. The toes are pointed downward.

PERFORMANCE
While maintaining a firm grip, lift the legs and feet backward and upward into an arch position. Then, swing the legs and feet downward, forward, and upward to assume a pike position. Throughout the entire process keep the arms locked and the shoulders positioned directly above the hands. Make the shoulders the fulcrum of the swing. At the height of the forward swing, with the hips and legs above the bars, push down on the far bar with the far hand and swing the body over the near bar. The back of the body passes over the bar. After the body passes over the bar, lower the legs and feet and land in an upright position on the balls of the feet with the knees bent and the outside arm extended sideward at shoulder level. The weight is balanced above the balls of the feet. At the same time, grasp the near bar with the far hand as the inside hand releases the grip.

FINISHING POSITION
End in a standing position by straightening the legs and lowering the heels to the mat. At the same time, lower the outside arm to place the arm at the side of the body. Also, release the grip of the far hand on the near bar and place the far arm at the side of the body. The body is straight up and down with the head level and the eyes focused forward.

IMPORTANT TEACHING SUGGESTIONS

1) Take time in the introductory lesson to discuss the mechanics of the Rear Dismount and follow-up with a demonstration of the dismount by yourself or by a skilled student. If possible, reinforce the discussion and demonstration with a Rear Dismount chart and/or a related audiovisual aid.

2) Take time in the introductory lesson to individually assess the proper execution of the dismount and make necessary corrections, if needed.

3) Teach the Straight Arm Support (refer to page 78 for teaching guidelines) and the Swing (refer to page 81 for teaching guidelines) as lead-up stunts to the Rear Dismount.

4) Emphasize the need to perform the dismount over a well matted area.

5) Stress the importance of using the overhand grip.

6) Make certain the students understand the importance of using a firm grip throughout the performance of the dismount.

7) Stress the need to keep the arms locked and the shoulders directly above the hands throughout the performance of the backward and forward swings.

8) Discuss the term "fulcrum" and relate it to the position of the shoulders throughout the performance of the backward and forward swings.

9) Tell the students to bend at the waist as the legs swing forward and upward to assume the pike position.

10) Discuss the term "balance" and relate it to the equal swinging motion of the legs and feet in back of and in front of the body.

11) Tell the students to keep the toes pointed throughout the backward and forward swings.

12) Stress the need to swing the legs and hips forward and upward above the bars to be able to swing the body over the near bar.

13) Make certain the students swing the body over the near bar at the height of the forward swing.

14) Emphasize the need to push down with a lot of force on the far bar with the far hand to help the body pass over the near bar.

15) Discuss the transfer of grips made with the far hand going from the far bar to the near bar.

16) Tell the students to keep the legs together throughout the entire performance of the Rear Dismount.

17) Stress the need to swing the body over the near bar and not allow it to come down on top of the bar.

18) Emphasize proper landing technique: Land in an upright balanced position on the balls of the feet with the knees bent and the head level.

19) Talk about the need to land in a balanced, upright position with the weight centered above the balls of the feet.

20) Encourage the students to land with the outside arm extended sideward at shoulder level, then lower the arm to the side of the body to assume the proper finishing position.

21) Tell the students to use the far hand to create a steady landing during the time the hand grips the near bar.

22) Tell the students to release the grip of the far hand on the near bar only after balance is maintained upon landing.

23) Discuss the "polished" look of the finishing position by having the body straight up and down, heels on the mat, arms at the sides of the body, head level, and the eyes focused forward.

24) Assist students, if needed.

SPOTTING HINTS

Position yourself next to the parallel bars while being slightly in front of and to the side of the student. Be on the opposite side where the dismount will be performed. Grasp the student's closest upper arm near the student's arm pit with your back hand. The fingers of your back hand circle toward the front of the student's upper arm. On your signal, instruct the student to perform the Rear Dismount. Give the student the necessary support with your back hand to be able to maintain balance and stability while swinging the legs and feet backward and forward. When the student is close to reaching the highest point of the forward swing, grasp the back of the student's closest leg midway between the knee and the hip with your front hand by having your fingers circle toward the front of the student's leg with your thumb circling in back of the student's leg. Help the student swing the legs and feet high enough on the forward swing to safely swing the legs and hips above the bars. Assuming the student's forward swing is under control, and the legs and hips are higher than the bars, maintain a firm grip on the student's closest leg with your front hand and push the student's legs and body over the opposite bar. Release your grip on the student's closest leg after the student's body passes over the opposite bar. Maintain your grip on the student's closest upper arm with your back hand throughout the process of the student changing grips from one bar to the other. Release your grip on the student's upper arm after the student has successfully and safely landed using the proper landing technique.

If the student is unable to swing the legs and hips higher than the bars on the forward swing or if the student is unable to keep the body in the proper position throughout the backward and forward swings, do not force the student to perform the Rear Dismount. Instead, encourage the student to practice the Swing to be able to maintain balance and stability during the swinging movements while trying to reach a height higher than the bars on the forward swing. When the student achieves success on the forward swing, while maintaining the proper position throughout the backward and forward swings, give the student another opportunity to perform the Rear Dismount while being spotted.

Make certain you position yourself properly so as not to place undue pressure on your lower back or other potentially weak areas of your body. Do not overspot. Instead, have the student perform the Rear Dismount by providing a minimum amount of spotting necessary for a successful and safe performance of the dismount. Continue to give individualized assistance using the preceding method. If possible, encourage the student to practice the Rear Dismount without assistance.

FORWARD SWING AT END DISMOUNT

STARTING POSITION
Begin in a forward Straight Arm Support position at the end of the parallel bars. The arms are straight and positioned along the sides of the body. The head is level and the body is straight up and down with the shoulders positioned directly above the hands. The toes are pointed downward.

PERFORMANCE
While maintaining a firm grip, lift the legs and feet backward and upward into an arch position. Then, swing the legs and feet downward, forward, and upward while bending at the waist. Throughout this entire process keep the arms locked and the shoulders positioned directly above the hands. Make the shoulders the fulcrum of the swing. At the height of the forward swing, push-off the ends of the parallel bars in an upward and forward direction. Lower the legs and feet and land in an upright position on the balls of the feet with the knees bent and arms extended side-ward at shoulder level. The weight is balanced above the balls of the feet.

FINISHING POSITION
End in a standing position by straightening the legs and lowering the heels to the mat. At the same time, lower the arms to place them at the sides of the body. The body is straight up and down with the head level and the eyes focused forward.

IMPORTANT TEACHING SUGGESTIONS

1) Take time in the introductory lesson to discuss the mechanics of the Forward Swing At End Dismount and follow-up with a demonstration of the dismount by yourself or by a skilled student. If possible, reinforce the discussion and demonstration with a Forward Swing At End Dismount chart and/or a related audiovisual aid.

2) Take time in the introductory lesson to individually assess the proper execution of the dismount and make necessary corrections, if needed.

3) Teach the Straight Arm Support (refer to page 78 for teaching guidelines) and the Swing (refer to page 81 for teaching guidelines) as lead-up stunts to the Forward Swing At End Dismount.

4) Emphasize the need to perform the dismount above a well matted area.

5) Stress the importance of using the overhand grip.

6) Make certain the students understand the importance of using a firm grip throughout the performance of the dismount.

7) Stress the need to keep the arms locked and the shoulders directly above the hands throughout the performance of the backward and forward swings.

8) Discuss the term "fulcrum" and relate it to the position of the shoulders throughout the performance of the backward and forward swings.

9) Tell the students to bend at the waist as the legs and feet swing forward and upward to assume the pike position.

10) Discuss the term "balance" and relate it to the equal swinging motion of the legs and feet in back of and in front of the body.

11) Tell the students to keep the toes pointed throughout the backward and forward swings.

12) Stress the need to push-off the ends of the parallel bars in an upward and forward direction at the height of the forward swing.

13) Emphasize the proper landing technique: Land in an upright, balanced position on the balls of the feet with the knees bent and the head level.

14) Talk about the need to land in a balanced, upright position with the weight centered above the balls of the feet.

15) Encourage the students to land with the arms extended sideward at shoulder level then lower them to the sides of the body to assume the proper finishing position.

16) Discuss the "polished" look of the finishing position by having the body straight up and down, heels on the mat, arms at the sides of the body, head level, and eyes focused forward.

17) Assist students, if necessary.

SPOTTING HINTS

Position yourself next to the end of the parallel bars while being directly beside and facing the student. Grasp the student's near wrist with your front hand and grasp the back of the student's closest upper arm near the student's arm pit with your back hand. The fingers of your back hand circle toward the front of the student's upper arm. On your signal, instruct the student to perform the Forward Swing At End Dismount. Give the student the necessary support with your back hand to be able to maintain balance and stability while swinging the legs and feet backward and forward. When the student reaches the highest point on the forward swing, release your grips to allow the student freedom while being airborne. Move forward along side of the student as he/she travels forward through the air. Stop beside the student during the landing but be out of the way of the student's extended arms. Put your front hand in front of the student's chest and put your back hand behind the student in the area of the student's shoulder blades. Be prepared to assist the student if he/she loses balance and begins to fall forward, backward, or sideward. Once the student assumes the finishing position, give verbal cues to remind the student to have the body straight up and down, heels on the mat, arms at the sides of the body, head level, and the eyes focused forward.

Make certain you position yourself properly so as not to place undue pressure on your lower back or other potentially weak areas of your body. Do not overspot. Instead, have the student perform the Forward Swing At End Dismount by providing a minimum amount of spotting necessary to allow for a successful and safe performance of the dismount. Continue to give individualized assistance using the preceding method. If possible, encourage the student to practice the Forward Swing At End Dismount without assistance.

BACKWARD SWING AT END DISMOUNT

STARTING POSITION
Begin in a backward Straight Arm Support position at the end of the parallel bars. The arms are straight and positioned along the sides of the body. The head is level and the body is straight up and down with the shoulders positioned directly above the hands. The toes are pointed downward.

PERFORMANCE
While maintaining a firm grip, lift the legs forward and upward while bending at the waist into a pike position. Then, swing the legs and feet backward and upward into an arch position. Throughout this entire process keep the arms locked and the shoulders positioned directly above the hands. Make the shoulders the fulcrum of the swing. At the height of the backward swing, push-off the ends of the parallel bars in an upward and backward direction. Lower the legs and feet and land in an upright position on the balls of the feet with the knees bent and arms extended sideward at shoulder level. The weight is balanced above the balls of the feet.

FINISHING POSITION
End in a standing position by straightening the legs and lowering the heels to the mat. At the same time, lower the arms to place them at the sides of the body. The body is straight up and down with the head level and the eyes focused forward.

IMPORTANT TEACHING SUGGESTIONS

1) Take time in the introductory lesson to discuss the mechanics of the Backward Swing At End Dismount and follow-up with a demonstration of the dismount by yourself or by a skilled student. If possible, reinforce the discussion and demonstration with a Backward Swing At End Dismount chart and/or a related audiovisual aid.

2) Take time in the introductory lesson to individually assess the proper execution of the dismount and make necessary corrections, if needed.

3) Teach the Straight Arm Support (refer to page 78 for teaching guidelines) and the Swing (refer to page 81 for teaching guidelines) as lead-up stunts to the Backward Swing At End Dismount.

4) Emphasize the need to perform the dismount above a well matted area.

5) Stress the importance of using the overhand grip.

6) Make certain the students understand the importance of using a firm grip throughout the performance of the dismount.

7) Stress the need to keep the arms locked and the shoulders directly above the hands throughout the performance of the forward and backward swings.

8) Discuss the term "fulcrum" and relate it to the position of the shoulders throughout the performance of the forward and backward swings.

9) Tell the students to bend at the waist as the legs and feet swing forward and upward to assume a pike position.

10) Discuss the term "balance" and relate it to the equal swinging motion of the legs and feet in front of and in back of the body.

11) Tell the students to keep the toes pointed throughout the forward and backward swings.

12) Stress the need to push-off the ends of the parallel bars in an upward and backward direction at the height of the backward swing.

13) Emphasize the proper landing technique: Land in an upright balanced position on the balls of the feet with the knees bent and the head level.

14) Talk about the need to land in a balanced upright position with the weight centered above the balls of the feet.

15) Encourage the students to land with the arms extended sideward at shoulder level then lower them to the sides of the body to assume the proper finishing position.

16) Discuss the "polished" look of the finishing position by having the body straight up and down, heels on the mat, arms at the sides of the body, head level, and the eyes focused forward.

17) Assist students, if necessary.

SPOTTING HINTS

Position yourself next to the end of the parallel bars while being directly beside and facing the student. Grasp the student's near wrist with your back hand and grasp the back of the student's closest upper arm near the student's arm pit with your front hand. The fingers of your front hand circle toward the front of the student's upper arm. On your signal, instruct the student to perform the Backward Swing At End Dismount. Give the student the necessary support with your front hand to be able to maintain balance and stability while swinging the legs and feet forward and backward. When the student reaches the highest point of the backward swing, release your grips to allow the student freedom while being airborne. Move forward along side the student as he/she travels backward through the air. Stop beside the student during the landing but be out of the way of the student's extended arms. Put your front hand in front of the student's shoulder blades and put your back hand in front of the student's chest. Be prepared to assist the student if he/she loses balance and begins to fall forward, backward, or sideward. Once the student assumes the finishing position, give verbal cues to remind the student to have the body straight up and down, heels on the mat, arms at the sides of the body, head level, and the eyes focused forward.

Make certain you position yourself properly so as not to place undue pressure on your lower back or other potentially weak areas of your body. <u>Do not</u> overspot. Instead, have the student perform the Backward Swing At End Dismount by providing a minimum amount of spotting necessary to allow for a successful and safe performance of the dismount. Continue to give individualized assistance using the preceding method. If possible, encourage the student to practice the Backward Swing At End Dismount without assistance.

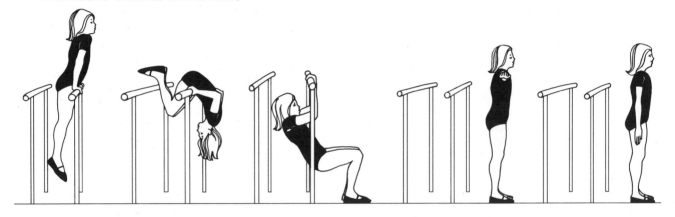

FORWARD ROLL OVER SIDE DISMOUNT

STARTING POSITION
Begin in a balanced straight arm support position in the middle of and against the inside of the near bar. The arms are straight and positioned along the sides of the body. The head is level and the body is straight up and down with the shoulders positioned slightly in front of the bar. The hips are pressed against the bar and the toes are pointed.

PERFORMANCE
Bend at the waist while tucking the chin, rounding the back, bending the arms, and bending the legs. The body assumes a semi-tuck position. Do a forward roll over the bar. Maintain the semi-tuck position and allow the feet to be placed on the mat. Pull forward and upward with the hands while ducking the head under the near bar to begin to place the body in a standing position. After balance is attained in a standing position, release the grips and extend the arms sideward at shoulder level.

FINISHING POSITION
End in a standing position by straightening the legs and lowering the heels to the mat. At the same time, lower the arms to place them at the sides of the body. The body is straight up and down with the head level and the eyes focused forward.

IMPORTANT TEACHING SUGGESTIONS

1) Take time in the introductory lesson to discuss the mechanics of the Forward Roll Over Side Dismount and follow-up with a demonstration of the dismount by yourself or by a skilled student. If possible, reinforce the discussion and demonstration with a Forward Roll Over Side Dismount chart and/or a related audiovisual aid.

2) Take time in the introductory lesson to individually assess the proper execution of the dismount and make necessary corrections, if needed.

3) Emphasize the need to perform the dismount above a well matted area.

4) Stress the importance of using the overhand grip.

5) Make certain the students understand the importance of using a firm grip throughout the performance of the dismount.

6) Stress the need to bend slowly at the waist while tucking the chin, rounding the back, bending the arms, and bending the legs. These movements must be slow and completely under control.

7) Tell the students that it might be necessary to tilt the legs sideward to be able to safely perform the forward roll over the bar without the feet or legs striking the far bar.

8) Explain how the hands turn on the bar while maintaining the overhand grip position throughout the performance of the dismount.

9) Discuss the need to pull upward and forward while ducking the head under the near bar to assume a standing position.

10) Tell the students to maintain the grip on the near bar until a balanced, standing position is attained.

11) Encourage the students to extend the arms sideward at shoulder level then lower them to the sides of the body to assume the proper finishing position.

12) Discuss the "polished" look of the finishing position by having the body straight up and down, heels on the mat, arms at the sides of the body, head level, and the eyes focused forward.

13) Assist students, if necessary.

SPOTTING HINTS

Position yourself beside the near bar and facing the student. Grasp the student's near wrist with your inside hand. On your signal, instruct the student to perform the Forward Roll Over Side Dismount. As the student bends at the waist to begin the forward roll over the bar, place your outside hand behind the student's head in the area of the student's upper back. Give the student the necessary support with your outside hand to perform the initial rolling movement over the bar. Maintain a firm grip on the student's near wrist with your inside hand as the student's hand begins to turn around the bar. When the student's head passes below the bar in the continual movement of the forward roll, start to reposition your outside hand by sliding it down the center of the student's back to place it behind the student's knees. Throughout the repositioning of your outside hand, give the student the necessary support and lift to be able to complete the forward roll movement and to place the feet safely on the mat.

After the student has placed his/her feet on the mat and starts to pull forward and upward with the hands, take your outside hand away from the student's knees. Keep your grip on the student's near wrist with your inside hand and help the student to pull and lift his/her body while ducking the head under the bar to place the body in a standing position. Release your grip once the student has attained a balanced standing position.

Make certain you position yourself properly so as not to place undue pressure on your lower back or other potentially weak areas of your body. Do not overspot. Instead, have the student perform the Forward Roll Over Side Dismount by providing a minimum amount of spotting necessary to allow for a successful and safe performance of the dismount. Continue to give individualized assistance using the preceding method. If possible, encourage the student to practice the Forward Roll Over Side Dismount without assistance.

Chapter – 8

PARALLEL BARS PROGRESSION CHART (K-8)

INTRODUCTION

Use the following Parallel Bars Progression Chart as a guide for the introduction of Parallel Bars Stunts, Turns, Mounts, and Dismounts at the K-8 levels; however, do not feel compelled to accept the Chart as the final word. Each physical education program is unique in itself. Physical education instructors with limited backgrounds in parallel bars instruction might feel more comfortable to introduce certain skills at a later grade level; whereas, physical education instructors with strong backgrounds in parallel bars instruction might feel comfortable to introduce certain skills at an earlier grade level. For example, I attempt to individualize my parallel bars instructional program by creating ability level groupings within each class at every grade level. In so doing, I introduce Parallel Bars Stunts, Turns, Mounts, and Dismounts differently throughout all grade levels. There are many other factors to consider when determining the appropriate grade level at which to introduce specific Parallel Bars Stunts, Turns, Mounts, and Dismounts including weekly physical education allotment time for each grade level or class, availability and the number of parallel bars, student backgrounds and gymnastics experiences, local physical education program guidelines and/or restraints, number of lessons/weeks allotted to the parallel bars/gymnastics unit, and parental/volunteer help to assist with the parallel bars/gymnastics instruction. Look closely at your physical education program and select or establish a Parallel Bars Progression Chart that best fits your program and student needs.

PARALLEL BARS PROGRESSION CHART (K-8)

PARALLEL BARS STUNTS	K	1	2	3	4	5	6	7	8
Hand Knee Hang	X	X	X	X	X	X	X	X	X
Skin The Cat		X*	X	X	X	X	X	X	X
Bird's Nest		X*	X	X	X	X	X	X	X
Tuck Hang			X	X	X	X	X	X	X
Pike Hang				X	X	X	X	X	X
Inverted Hang				X	X	X	X	X	X
Straight Arm Support			X	X	X	X	X	X	X
Swing				X	X	X	X	X	X
Straddle Seat		X	X	X	X	X	X	X	X
Left Side Seat				X	X	X	X	X	X
Right Side Seat				X	X	X	X	X	X
Traveling Straddle Seat				X	X	X	X	X	X
Hand Walk Forward				X	X	X	X	X	X
Hand Walk Backward				X	X	X	X	X	X
Straight Arm Support Dip				X	X	X	X	X	X
V-Seat				X	X	X	X	X	X
Crouch Position				X	X	X	X	X	X
Front Leaning Rest				X	X	X	X	X	X
Knee Scale				X	X	X	X	X	X

* Give permission to students to practice the two parallel bars stunts with asterisks on an individual basis. For further clarification refer to the following sections within this book: Skin The Cat (pages 102 and 103) and Bird's Nest (page 104).

	K	1	2	3	4	5	6	7	8
PARALLEL BARS TURNS									
Straddle Seat Turn					X	X	X	X	X
Side Seat Turn					X	X	X	X	X
Straight Arm Support Turn						X	X	X	X
PARALLEL BARS MOUNTS									
Straight Arm Support At End Mount					X	X	X	X	X
Straight Arm Support At Side Mount					X	X	X	X	X
Straight Arm Support In The Middle Mount					X	X	X	X	X
Straddle Seat At End Mount					X	X	X	X	X
Straddle Seat In The Middle Mount					X	X	X	X	X
Left Side Seat At End Mount					X	X	X	X	X
Right Side Seat At End Mount					X	X	X	X	X
Forward Roll Into Hand Knee Hang Mount					X	X	X	X	X
Back Pull Over Into Straddle Seat Mount					X	X	X	X	X
PARALLEL BARS DISMOUNTS									
Forward Swing at End Dismount					X	X	X	X	X
Backward Swing at End Dismount					X	X	X	X	X
Forward Roll Over Side Dismount					X	X	X	X	X
Rear Dismount					X	X	X	X	X
Front Dismount					X	X	X	X	X

Chapter - 9

ASSESSMENTS

INTRODUCTION

The Assessments Chapter includes assessment samples for the three educational domains of Psycho Motor, Cognitive, and Affective. Each sample includes Teaching Suggestions along with a detailed explanation of the specific assessment.

Psycho Motor Domain
PARALLEL BARS STUNTS CHECK SHEET
(Example For Grade 5)

_____ SWING

_____ TRAVELING STRADDLE SEAT

_____ KNEE SCALE

_____ HAND WALK FORWARD

_____ SKIN THE CAT

_____ BIRD'S NEST

_____ PIKE HANG

_____ INVERTED HANG

TEACHING SUGGESTIONS FOR THE PARALLEL BARS STUNTS CHECK SHEET

1) Use the Parallel Bars Stunts Check Sheet beginning with students in the third grade. Modify the Parallel Bars Stunts Check Sheet to list parallel bars stunts taught at each grade level.

2) Hand out the Parallel Bars Stunts Check Sheets at the beginning of each class period and collect them at the end of each class period. Provide a pencil for each student or each small group of students. Ask each student to always place the Parallel Bars Stunts Check Sheet and pencil against the nearest wall or at a teacher designated location close to the parallel bars. Also, consider hanging pencils from string and taping the string at a few places on the gymnasium wall closest to the parallel bars. Ask the students to record with the hanging pencils.

3) Introduce a group of parallel bars stunts and allow time for practice and teacher assistance. Afterward, observe each student performing the group of parallel bars stunts. If the student performs one, a few, or all the stunts correctly then have the student place a check mark (or an X) in front of the mastered parallel bars stunt or stunts.

4) If time permits, provide time at the end of each lesson to give students additional opportunities to achieve checks for non-mastered parallel bars stunts.

5) Include a parallel bars station within the follow-up gymnastic station lessons and have the Parallel Bars Stunts Check Sheets available for the students to

continue practicing mastered and non-mastered parallel bars stunts. Plan to spend a few minutes within each class observing the progress of the students. Continue to give check marks.

6) Make the standards for check marks progressively more difficult for students throughout the grade levels on appropriate parallel bars stunts.

7) At the end of the parallel bars/gymnastic unit, give a circled check mark to a stunt for which the student practiced diligently to learn but didn't achieve the standard. It is a good idea to reward a student for sincere and dedicated effort. Share the purpose of the circled check mark with all students. The circled check mark can be a tremendous motivating instrument for students who have personal reasons for not reaching the top, but who are students who _always_ produce their personal best.

8) Consider using check sheets for the parallel bars turns, mounts, and dismounts especially for students in the sixth, seventh, and eighth grades.

Psycho Motor Domain
PARALLEL BARS ABILITY LEVEL ROUTINES

TEACHING SUGGESTIONS

1) Use the Parallel Bars Ability Level Routines beginning with students in the fourth grade. Modify the parallel bars routines to fit your parallel bars/gymnastics unit, if necessary.

2) Make a copy of each routine and have the routines available near the parallel bars for reciprocal teaching among students or for your use with the students.

3) Post a check sheet for each class on a wall near the parallel bars and include the names of all the students with corresponding columns for the five Parallel Bars Ability Level Routines.

4) Beginning with the first routine, have the student place a check mark next to his/her name within the first column to show mastery of the routine. The check mark signifies that the student performed the routine to the best of his/her ability without any modifications. Have the student progress through the remaining four routines following the same procedure, if possible.

5) Beginning with the first routine, have the student place a check mark with a circle around it next to his/her name within the first column to show mastery of the routine. The circled check mark signifies the student performed the routine to the best of his/her ability with at least one modification. Have the student progress through the remaining four routines following the same procedure, if necessary.

6) Encourage all students to attempt all routines, or as many as possible, without modifications; however, be aware that some students may not be capable of an "average" to "above average" level of performance due to a physical limitation, overweight, fear, lack of upper body, arm, and/or abdominal strength. Praise all performances regardless of ability level assuming the students were on task and gave their best efforts.

PARALLEL BARS ABILITY LEVEL ROUTINES

Level-1
    Straight Arm Support In The Middle Mount
    Swing
    Straddle Seat
    Swing into a **Left Side Seat**
    Swing into a **Right Side Seat**
    Swing into a **Straddle Seat**
    Move below bars into a **Hand Knee Hang**
    Bird's Nest
    Move above bars into a **Straddle Seat**
    Rear Dismount

Level-2
    Right Side Seat At End Mount
    Straight Arm Support
    Hand Walk Forward to the middle
    Swing
    Straddle Seat
    Crouch Position
    Straddle Seat
    V-Seat
    Move below bars into a **Skin The Cat**
    Bird's Nest
    Move above bars into a **Straddle Seat**
    Straight Arm Support
    Hand Walk Forward to the end
    Forward Swing At End Dismount

Level-3
    Straddle Seat At End Mount
    Traveling Straddle Seat to the middle
    Front Leaning Rest
    Knee Scale
    Straddle Seat
    Straddle Seat Turn
    Move below bars into a **Hand Knee Hang**
    Tuck Hang
    Pike Hang
    Inverted Hang
    Move above bars into a **Straddle Seat**
    Straight Arm Support
    Move into position to do a **Forward Roll Over**
    Side Dismount

Level-4
    Forward Roll Into Hand Knee Hang Mount
    Move into a **Tuck Hang**
    Pike Hang
    Inverted Hang
    Move above bars into a **Straddle Seat**
    Straight Arm Support
    Straight Arm Support Dip
    Straight Arm Support Turn
    Swing into a **Left Side Seat**
    Swing into a **Right Side Seat**
    Front Dismount

Level-5
Back Pullover Into Straddle Seat Mount
Straight Arm Support
Hand Walk Backward to the middle
Swing into a **Crouch Position**
Knee Scale
Right Side Seat
Side Seat Turn
Straddle Seat
Move below the bars into an **Inverted Hang**
Pike Hang
Tuck Hang
Bird's Nest
Skin The Cat
Jump into a **Straight Arm Support** in the middle
Traveling Straddle Seat to the end
Straight Arm Support
Straight Arm Support Turn
Backward Swing At End Dismount

Cognitive Domain

PARALLEL BARS STUNTS TEST

TEACHING SUGGESTIONS

1) Administer the Parallel Bars Stunts Test at the end of the parallel bars/gymnastics unit.

2) Use the Parallel Bars Stunts Test with students beginning in the fourth grade.

3) Make certain all parallel bars stunts appearing in the test have been discussed and practiced in class.

4) Use the test results to help determine each student's report card grade.

TEST INSTRUCTIONS

On the Parallel Bars Stunts Test that follows ask the students to circle the correct picture by matching the picture to the name of the parallel bars stunt that is written beside the number on the test. The parallel bars stunts are: 1) Front Leaning Rest; 2) Tuck Hang; 3) Knee Scale; 4) Hand Knee Hang; 5) Straddle Seat; 6) Pike Hang; 7) Crouch Position; 8) Bird's Nest; 9) Right Side Seat; and 10) Inverted Hang. (The answers to the Parallel Bars Stunts Test are: 1 = B; 2 = A; 3 = C; 4 = B; 5 = C; 6 = A; 7 = B; 8 = A; 9 = C; and 10 = B.)

PARALLEL BARS STUNTS TEST

NAME_____

TEACHER_____

1) FRONT LEANING REST

A

B

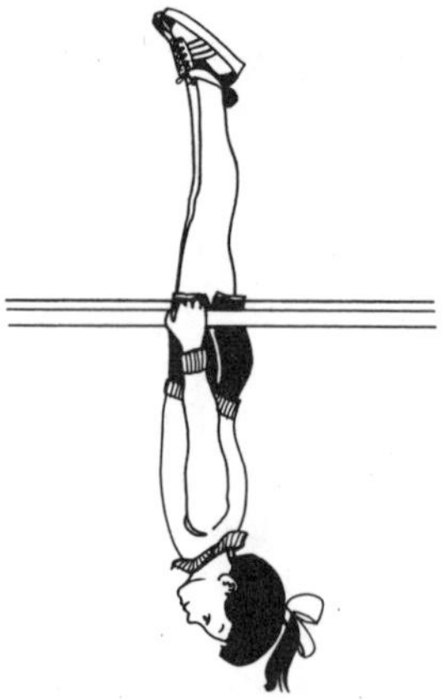

C

2) TUCK HANG

A

B

C

3) KNEE SCALE

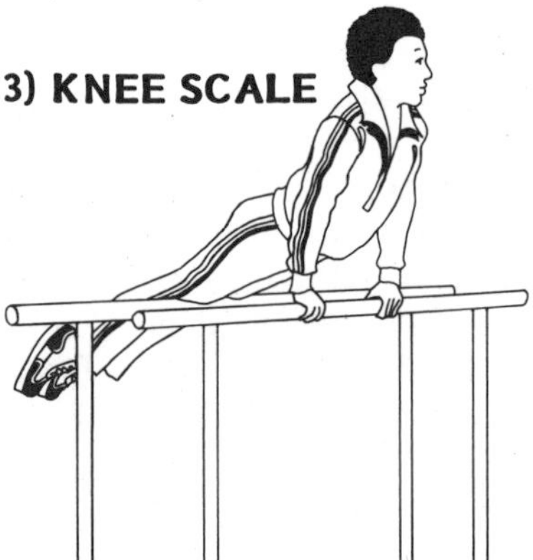

A

B

C

4) HAND KNEE HANG

A

B

C

5) STRADDLE SEAT

A

B

C

6) PIKE HANG

A

B

C

7) CROUCH POSITION

A

B

C

8) BIRD'S NEST

A

B

C

9) RIGHT SIDE SEAT

A

B

C

10) INVERTED HANG

A

B

C

Cognitive Domain
PARALLEL BARS TEST

TEACHING SUGGESTIONS

1) Administer the test that follows at the end of the parallel bars/gymnastics unit.

2) Use the Parallel Bars Test beginning with students in the fourth grade.

3) Modify and/or change the test questions to fit your parallel bars/gymnastic unit.

4) Make certain all the information is discussed and/or practiced in class.

5) Tell the students at the beginning of the parallel bars/gymnastics unit that they will be given a written test at the end of the unit and the test results will be used to determine each student's report card grade.

TEST INSTRUCTIONS

On the Parallel Bars Test that follows ask the students to circle the correct letter of the word(s) that completes the sentence or answers the question best. The answers to the Test are: 1 = D; 2 = C; 3 = D; 4 = A; 5 = A; 6 = B; 7 = C; 8 = B; 9 = A; 10 = C; 11 = D; 12 = A; 13 = D; and 14 = C.

PARALLEL BARS TEST

1) A warm-up activity is important before beginning to use the parallel bars because it helps to:
     A) tighten muscles and body joints
     B) make the body tired
     C) create muscle cramps
     D) stretch muscles and body joints

2) A lot of strength is need in the_____ in order to hold and move the body above the parallel bars.
     A) Abdominal (stomach) area
     B) thighs
     C) upper body and arms
     D) ankles and feet

3) A Straddle Seat is performed on the parallel bars by placing:
     A) both legs over the left bar
     B) the legs between the bars
     C) both legs over the right bar
     D) one leg over each bar

4) The word mount means to:
     A) get onto the parallel bars
     B) stay away from the parallel bars
     C) get off the parallel bars
     D) share the parallel bars with a friend

5) During the swing the shoulders must stay directly_____ the hands.

    A) above
    B) below
    C) in front of
    D) in back of

6) A Skin The Cat is performed by traveling backward then forward in a:

    A) pike position
    B) tuck position
    C) inverted position
    D) straddle position

7) Which stunt is not performed below the parallel bars?

    A) Skin The Cat
    B) Tuck Hang
    C) Straight Arm Support
    D) Bird's Nest

8) The rear dismount means the_____ passes over the bar while performing the dismount.

    A) front
    B) rear
    C) stomach
    D) side

9) When someone is practicing the Swing in the center of the parallel bars, how many persons should be using the parallel bars?

    A) one
    B) three
    C) two
    D) four

10) A Bird's Nest is performed by hooking the toes on the bars_____ the student.

    A) in front of
    B) above
    C) behind
    D) below

11) The word dismount means to:

    A) hide under the parallel bars
    B) get onto the parallel bars
    C) sit on top of the parallel bars
    D) get off the parallel bars

12) The Straddle Seat Turn is performed by being in the_____ position.

    A) straddle seat
    B) straight arm support
    C) crouch
    D) side seat

13) Which stunt is not performed above the parallel bars?

    A) Traveling Straddle Seat
    B) Hand Walk Forward
    C) Straight Arm Support Dip
    D) Inverted Hang

14) The safest body parts to land on when dismounting off the parallel bars are the_____.

      A) knees
      B) buttocks
      C) feet
      D) hands

15) Select one of our parallel bars stunts and explain how you would teach it to a younger brother or sister. Be certain to include a beginning position and an ending position.

Cognitive Domain
PARALLEL BARS ROUTINE WORKSHEET

TEACHING SUGGESTIONS

1) Use the Parallel Bars Routine Worksheet that follows beginning with students in the fourth grade.

2) Make certain boys and girls have the opportunity to develop a Parallel Bars Routine. Do not exclude the girls from this worthwhile learning experience.

3) Discuss the development of a Parallel Bars Routine with the students. Use a chalkboard, large piece of paper, bulletin board display, or similar instructional aid to supplement the presentation.

4) Create a Parallel Bars Routine as a sample for the students. Use the Parallel Bars Routine Worksheet that follows these Teaching Suggestions.

5) Have the students develop the Parallel Bars Routines in a class session or have the students develop the Parallel Bars Routines as a take home assignment.

6) Make certain you include the pictures of the Stunts, Turns, Mounts, and Dismounts as a supplemental page or supplemental pages of the Parallel Bars Routine Worksheet. Use the illustrations that follow the sample Worksheet.

7) Collect the Parallel Bars Routines and review them outside the class setting, if possible. Be positive with your comments.

8) Give each student ample time to practice his/her Parallel Bars Routine before showing it to you.

9) Have each student memorize his/her Parallel Bars Routine prior to showing it to you.

10) Establish clear cut guidelines for grading the Parallel Bars Routines. Depending on the grade level, look for perfection of movements in a progressive manner through the grade levels.

11) Make certain you consider one's effort, attitude toward the assignment, whether or not one memorized the Parallel Bars Routine, and the complexity of the Parallel Bars Routine in determining the final grade.

12) Give all students the opportunity to share their Parallel Bars Routines with fellow classmates; however, <u>do not</u> force a student to share his/her Parallel Bars Routine if the student chooses not to do so.

13) Place the grade and comments on the completed Parallel Bars Routine. Encourage the students to take their Parallel Bars Routines home to share them with their parents/guardians.

14) Use the Parallel Bars Routine Worksheet grade to help determine each student's report card grade.

PARALLEL BARS ROUTINE WORKSHEET

NAME _____ TEACHER _____ GRADE_____

Mount _____

Stunts (above or below the bars—include at least three Stunts)

_____

_____

_____

_____

_____

Turn _____

Stunts (above or below bars—opposite of 1st group of Stunts—include at least 3 Stunts)

_____

_____

_____

_____

_____

Dismount _____

Parallel Bars Mounts

STRAIGHT ARM SUPPORT
AT END MOUNT

STRAIGHT ARM SUPPORT
AT SIDE MOUNT

STRAIGHT ARM SUPPORT
IN THE MIDDLE MOUNT

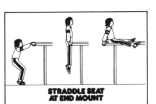

STRADDLE SEAT
AT END MOUNT

STRADDLE SEAT
IN THE MIDDLE MOUNT

LEFT SIDE SEAT
AT END MOUNT

RIGHT SIDE SEAT
AT END MOUNT

FORWARD ROLL INTO
HAND KNEE HANG MOUNT

BACK PULL OVER INTO
STRADDLE SEAT MOUNT

Parallel Bars Stunts

STRAIGHT ARM
SUPPORT

SWING

STRADDLE SEAT

TRAVELING STRADDLE SEAT

LEFT SIDE SEAT

RIGHT SIDE SEAT

FRONT LEANING
REST

CROUCH POSITION

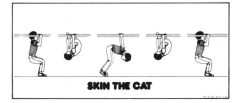

SKIN THE CAT

BIRD'S NEST

BACK ARCH

TUCK HANG

PIKE HANG

HAND WALK FORWARD

STRAIGHT ARM
SUPPORT DIP

HAND WALK BACKWARD

INVERTED HANG

V-SEAT

KNEE SCALE

HAND KNEE HANG

Parallel Bars Turns

Parallel Bars Dismounts

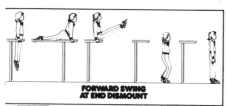

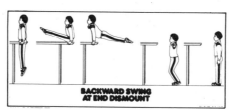

Affective Domain
PARALLEL BARS STUNTS DRAWING AND COLORING ACTIVITY

TEACHING SUGGESTIONS

1) Have the students do the drawing and coloring activity toward the end of or at the end of the parallel bars/gymnastics unit.

2) Use the drawing and coloring activity with students in grade one, grade two, and grade three.

3) Consider asking the classroom teacher(s) to give the students time within their daily schedule to do the drawing and coloring activity. The drawing and coloring could be a welcomed rainy day activity or quiet time activity. If not, do the drawing and coloring activity in the gymnasium or, if appropriate, in the classroom.

4) Display selected finished drawings or, if possible, display all drawings in the gymnasium, hallway(s), cafeteria, and/or classroom(s).

5) Encourage the students to take the drawings home after the display period to share with parents/guardians.

INSTRUCTIONS

Student instructions for the Parallel Bars Stunts Drawing And Coloring Activity should be something similar to: "Draw a picture of your favorite Parallel Bars Stunt and color it."

Affective Domain
PERSONAL FEELINGS CHECK SHEET FOR PARALLEL BARS STUNTS

TEACHING SUGGESTIONS

1) Use the check sheet that follows to help develop and stress the importance of being honest about one's ability level.

2) Use the check sheet beginning with students in the third grade. Modify the check sheet to list the parallel bars stunts taught at each grade level.

3) Administer the check sheet at the beginning of the parallel bars/gymnastics unit for guidance in setting up a parallel bars stunts unit to reach individual and class needs.

4) Share the check sheet at the end of the parallel bars/gymnastics unit to help evaluate the success of the unit and to help plan for next year's parallel bars/-gymnastics unit.

5) Tell the students that the recordings on the check sheets will be kept in confidence.

6) Tell the students that the check sheet responses will not affect their physical education grade.

7) Emphasize your role as a teacher, helper, and friend. Share your feelings with the students about the importance of the check sheet in helping you to develop a parallel bars stunts unit to best fit their individual and class needs.

8) Consider using check sheets for the parallel bars turns, mounts, and dismounts especially for students in the sixth, seventh, and eighth grades.

NAME _____

TEACHER _____

GRADE _____

PERSONAL FEELINGS CHECK SHEET FOR PARALLEL BARS STUNTS

	I feel I can perform the stunt.	I feel I need help with the stunt.	I am afraid to perform the stunt.
Hand Knee Hang			
Skin The Cat			
Bird's Nest			
Tuck Hang			
Pike Hang			
Inverted Hang			
Straight Arm Support			
Swing			
Straddle Seat			
Traveling Straddle Seat			
Hand Walk Forward			
Hand Walk Backward			
Left Side Seat			
Right Side Seat			
Straight Arm Support Dip			
Front Leaning Rest			

Place a check mark in the box that best fits your feelings for each stunt. Please be honest!

Chapter - 10

MOTIVATIONAL IDEAS

INTRODUCTION

The Motivational Ideas Chapter includes fifteen examples of ways to help motivate student performance and/or effort. Each example includes teaching suggestions along with a picture or graph to accompany the "motivational idea".

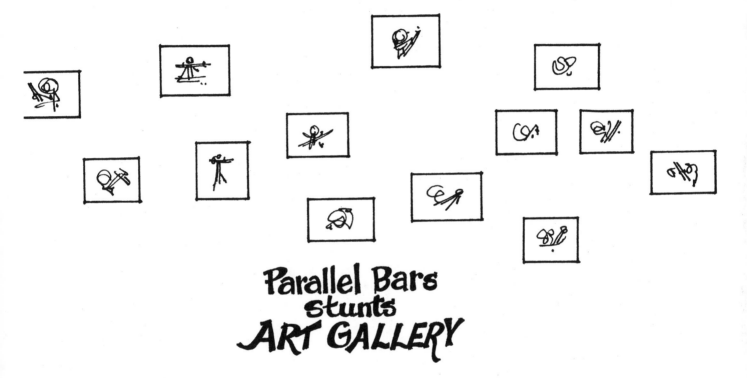

TEACHING SUGGESTIONS

1) Use the Parallel Bars Stunts Art Gallery to display the students' hand drawn colored parallel bars stunts drawings resulting from the Parallel Bars Stunts Drawing And Coloring Activity on page 146. Reward the students by posting the best or, if possible, post all deserving drawings regardless of student artistic abilities.

2) Place a star or some type of symbolic sticker on or next to each picture to indicate special recognition.

3) Announce the parallel bars stunts artists during morning or afternoon administrative announcements.

4) Present the drawings to the students after they are taken off the wall or bulletin board.

5) Encourage the students to take the drawings home after the display period to share with parents/guardians.

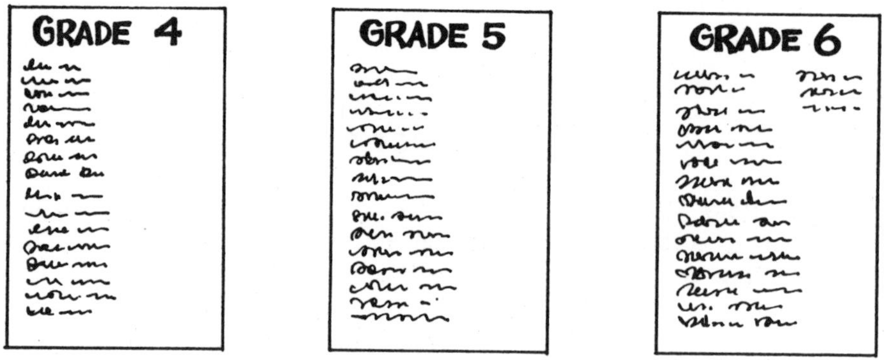

GRADE 4	GRADE 5	GRADE 6
(handwritten names)	*(handwritten names)*	*(handwritten names)*

Parallel Bars Stunts Club

TEACHING SUGGESTIONS

1) Use the Parallel Bars Stunts Club as a motivator for outstanding parallel bars stunts performance and effort.

2) Use the Parallel Bars Stunts Check Sheet on page 134 as a sample to develop your own list of parallel bars stunts for each grade level. Ask a student who receives check marks on all stunts to print/write his/her full name on the appropriate grade club sheet in red ink. A check mark symbolizes a mastered parallel bars stunt. Ask a student who receives a combination of check marks and circled check marks on all parallel bars stunts to print/write his/her full name on the appropriate grade club sheet in blue ink. A circled check mark symbolizes a parallel bars stunt that was not mastered but one that a student worked hard to achieve.

3) Give each student who makes the club a "special" Parallel Bars Stunts Club Certificate.

4) Announce the new club members during morning or afternoon administrative announcements.

5) Consider creating a club for the parallel bars turns, mounts, and dismounts especially for students in the sixth, seventh, and eighth grades.

Parallel Bars Stunts
STUDENT of the WEEK
Club

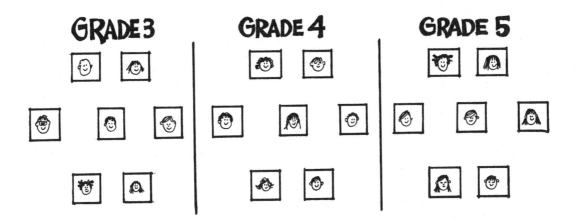

TEACHING SUGGESTIONS

1) Use the Parallel Bars Stunts Student Of The Week Club as a motivator for outstanding parallel bars stunts performance and effort.

2) Select a student at the end of the week from each classroom or grade level who has excelled in his/her parallel bars stunts performance and/or effort during the week. Take a photograph of the student and tape it under the specific grade level.

3) Give each student who makes the club a "special" Parallel Bars Stunts Student Of The Week Club Certificate.

4) Announce the new club members during the Friday afternoon administrative announcements.

5) Present the photographs to the students after the photographs are taken off the wall or bulletin board.

6) Encourage the students to take the photographs home after the display period to share with parents/guardians.

7) Consider a Student Of The Week Club for parallel bars turns, mounts, and dismounts especially for students in the sixth, seventh, and eighth grades.

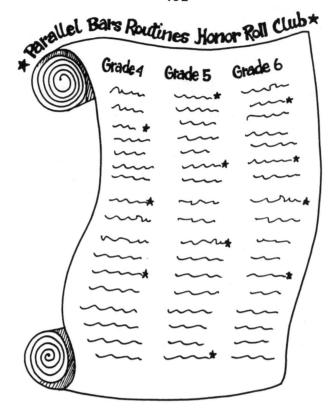

TEACHING SUGGESTIONS

1)   Use the Parallel Bars Routines Honor Roll Club as a motivator for exceptional parallel bars routines performance and effort.

2)   Use the parallel bars routines beginning on page 136. A student who performs the five parallel bars routines to the best of his/her ability without any modifications, prints/writes his/her name on the Parallel Bars Routines Honor Roll Club under the appropriate grade level. A student who performs the five parallel bars routines to the best of his/her ability with at least one modification, prints/writes his/her name on the Parallel Bars Routines Honor Roll Club under the appropriate grade level with an asterisk (*) at the end of the name.

3)   Give each student who makes the honor roll a "special" Parallel Bars Routines Honor Roll Club Certificate.

4)   Announce the new club members during morning or afternoon administrative announcements.

GRADE 3

Level 1 Walkers	Level 2 Walkers

GRADE 4

Level 1 Walkers	Level 2 Walkers

GRADE 5

Level 1 Walkers	Level 2 Walkers

HAND WALK FORWARD CLUB

TEACHING SUGGESTIONS

1) Use the Hand Walk Forward Club as a motivator for a successful performance.

2) Mark off a starting point near the beginning of the parallel bars. Also, mark off a Level-1 distance in the middle of the parallel bars and mark off a Level-2 distance near the end of the parallel bars.

3) Share the club requirements with the students and emphasize that the proper starting position, performance, and finishing position for the Hand Walk Forward must be used. See Hand Walk Forward beginning on page 88 for teaching guidelines. In order to meet the standard for the Level-1 walkers, a student must travel from the starting point to the Level-1 marker. Ask each student who passes the standard to print/write his/her full name on the appropriate grade level club sheet within the Level-1 Walkers section. In order to meet the standard for the Level-2 Walkers, a student must travel from the starting point to the Level-2 marker. Ask each student who passes the standard to print/write his/her full name on the appropriate grade level club sheet within the Level-2 Walkers section.

4) Take time within each class period to observe students who feel they are ready to attempt Level-1 or Level-2 of the Hand Walk Forward Club or use reciprocal teaching and have the students be responsible to observe each other's performances. Stress honesty and monitor the performances on an informal basis. Commend the students for being honest and responsible, if appropriate.

5) Give each student who makes the club a "special" Hand Walk Forward Club Certificate or sticker.

- 154 -

GRADE 3

Level 1 Walkers	Level 2 Walkers

GRADE 4

Level 1 Walkers	Level 2 Walkers

GRADE 5

Level 1 Walkers	Level 2 Walkers

HAND WALK BACKWARD CLUB

TEACHING SUGGESTIONS

1) Use the Hand Walk Backward Club as a motivator for a successful performance.

2) Mark off a starting point near the beginning of the parallel bars. Also, mark off a Level-1 distance one third the length of the parallel bars and mark off a Level-2 distance two thirds the length of the parallel bars. Do not allow the students to travel to the very end of the parallel bars.

3) Share the club requirements with the students and emphasize that the proper starting position, performance, and finishing position for the Hand Walk Backward must be used. See Hand Walk Backward beginning on page 90 for teaching guidelines. In order to meet the standard for the Level-1 walkers, a student must travel from the starting point to the Level-1 marker. Ask each student who passes the standard to print/write his/her full name on the appropriate grade level club sheet within the Level-1 Walkers section. In order to meet the standard for the Level-2 Walkers, a student must travel from the starting point to the Level-2 marker. Ask each student who passes the standard to print/write his/her full name on the appropriate grade level club sheet within the Level-2 Walkers section.

4) Take time within each class period to observe students who feel they are ready to attempt Level-1 or Level-2 of the Hand Walk Backward Club or use reciprocal teaching and have the students be responsible to observe each other's performances. Stress honesty and monitor the performances on an informal basis. Commend the students for being honest and responsible, if appropriate.

5) Give each student who makes the club a "special" Hand Walk Backward Club Certificate or sticker.

GRADE 4

BOYS	GIRLS
5	4

GRADE 5

BOYS	GIRLS
6	5

GRADE 6

BOYS	GIRLS
7	6

STRAIGHT ARM SUPPORT DIP CLUB

TEACHING SUGGESTIONS

1) Use the Straight Arm Support Dip Club as a motivator for a successful performance.

2) Share the club requirements with the students and emphasize that the proper Starting Position, Performance, and Finishing Position for each Straight Arm Support Dip must be used. See Straight Arm Support Dip beginning on page 79 for teaching guidelines.

3) Take time within each class period to observe students who feel they are ready to attempt the Straight Arm Support Dip Club or use reciprocal teaching and have the students be responsible to observe each other's performances. Stress honesty and monitor the performances on an informal basis. Commend the students for being honest and responsible, if appropriate.

4) Ask each student who passes the club requirements to print/write his/her full name on the appropriate grade level club sheet.

5) Give each student who makes the club a "special" Straight Arm Support Dip Club Certificate or sticker.

GRADE 4
BOYS	GIRLS
8	6

GRADE 5
BOYS	GIRLS
9	7

GRADE 6
BOYS	GIRLS
10	8

PUSH-UP CLUB

TEACHING SUGGESTIONS

1) Use the Push-Up Club as a motivator for a successful performance.

2) Share the club requirements with the students and emphasize that the proper Starting Position, Performance, and Finishing Position for each Push-Up must be used. See Push-Up beginning on page 39 for teaching guidelines.

3) Take time within each class period to observe students who feel they are ready to attempt the Push-Up Club or use reciprocal teaching and have the students be responsible to observe each other's performances. Stress honesty and monitor the performances on an informal basis. Commend the students for being honest and responsible, if appropriate.

4) Ask each student who passes the club requirements to print/write his/her full name on the appropriate grade level club sheet.

5) Give each student who makes the club a "special" Push-Up Club Certificate or sticker.

GRADE 3

BOYS	GIRLS
6	4

GRADE 4

BOYS	GIRLS
8	6

GRADE 5

BOYS	GIRLS
10	8

MODIFIED PUSH-UP CLUB

TEACHING SUGGESTIONS

1) Use the Modified Push-Up Club as a motivator for students who are unable to perform Push-Ups. These are students who are overweight, lack upper body and arm strength, or have a physical limitation in the lower extremities.

2) Share the club requirements with the students and emphasize that the proper Starting Position, Performance, and Finishing Position for each Modified Push-Up must be used. See Modified Push-Up beginning on page 41 for teaching guidelines.

3) Take time within each class period to observe students who feel they are ready to attempt the Modified Push-Up Club or use reciprocal teaching and have the students be responsible to observe each other's performances. Stress honesty and monitor the performances on an informal basis. Commend the students for being honest and responsible, if appropriate.

4) Ask each student who passes the club requirements to print/write his/her full name on the appropriate grade level club sheet.

5) Give each student who makes the club a "special" Modified Push-Up Club Certificate or sticker.

6) After a student makes the club have the student begin to perform Push-Ups (refer to page 39 for teaching guidelines). At first, have the student perform one Push-Up then perform Modified Push-Ups. If successful, increase the Push-Ups by one each time while lessening the number of Modified Push-Ups. Be patient and supportive with this kind of student and continually challenge the student to give his/her very best effort and encourage the student to perform to his/her maximum potential.

7) Challenge the student to begin to work toward attaining the performance level needed to make the Combination Push-Up Club (refer to page 158 for teaching guidelines).

- 158 -

GRADE 4

BOYS		GIRLS	
Modified Push Up	Push Up	Modified Push Up	Push Up
4	4	3	3

GRADE 5

BOYS		GIRLS	
Modified Push Up	Push Up	Modified Push Up	Push Up
5	4	4	3

GRADE 6

BOYS		GIRLS	
Modified Push Up	Push Up	Modified Push Up	Push Up
5	5	4	4

COMBINATION PUSH-UP CLUB

TEACHING SUGGESTIONS

1) Use the Combination Push-Up Club as a motivator for students who are unable to make the Push-Up Club but who have made the Modified Push-Up Club. These are students who are overweight or lack upper body and arm strength. The club is a stepping stone between the Modified Push-Up Club and the Push-Up Club.

2) Share the club requirements with the students and emphasize the proper Starting Position, Performance, and Finishing Position for each Modified Push-Up and Push-Up must be used. See Modified Push-Up beginning on page 41 for teaching guidelines and see Push-Up beginning on page 39 for teaching guidelines.

3) Take time within each class period to observe students who feel they are ready to attempt the Combination Push-Up Club or use reciprocal teaching and have the students be responsible to observe each other's performances. Stress honesty and monitor the performances on an informal basis. Commend the students for being honest and responsible, if appropriate.

4) Ask each student who passes the club requirements to print/write his/her full name on the appropriate grade level club sheet.

5) Give each student who makes the club a "special" Combination Push-Up Club Certificate or sticker.

6) After a student makes the club have the student begin to do all Push-Ups. Be patient and supportive with this kind of student and continually challenge the student to give his/her very best effort and encourage the student to perform to his/her maximum potential.

7) Challenge the student to begin to work toward attaining the performance level needed to make the Push-Up Club.

GRADE 4

BOYS	GIRLS
3	2

GRADE 5

BOYS	GIRLS
4	3

GRADE 6

BOYS	GIRLS
5	4

PULL-UP CLUB

TEACHING SUGGESTIONS

1) Use the Pull-Up Club as a motivator for a successful performance.

2) Share the club requirements with the students and emphasize that the proper Starting Position, Performance, and Finishing Position for each Pull-Up must be used. See Pull-Up on page 47 for teaching guidelines.

3) Take time within each class period to observe students who feel they are ready to attempt the Pull-Up Club or use reciprocal teaching and have the students be responsible to observe each other's performances. Stress honesty and monitor the performances on an informal basis. Commend the students for being honest and responsible, if appropriate.

4) Ask each student who passes the club requirements to print/write his/her full name on the appropriate grade level club sheet.

5) Give each student who makes the club a "special" Pull-Up Club Certificate or sticker.

GRADE 4

BOYS	GIRLS
3	2

GRADE 5

BOYS	GIRLS
4	3

GRADE 6

BOYS	GIRLS
5	4

CHIN-UP CLUB

TEACHING SUGGESTIONS

1) Use the Chin-Up Club as a motivator for a successful performance.

2) Share the club requirements with the students and emphasize that the proper Starting Position, Performance, and Finishing Position for each Chin-Up must be used. See Chin-Up on page 50 for teaching guidelines.

3) Take time within each class period to observe students who feel they are ready to attempt the Chin-Up or use reciprocal teaching and have the students be responsible to observe each other's performances. Stress honesty and monitor the performances on an informal basis. Commend the students for being honest and responsible, if appropriate.

4) Ask each student who passes the club requirements to print/write his/her full name on the appropriate grade level club sheet.

5) Give each student who makes the club a "special" Chin-Up Certificate or sticker.

GRADE 4

BOYS	GIRLS
5 seconds	4 seconds

GRADE 5

BOYS	GIRLS
8 seconds	6 seconds

GRADE 6

BOYS	GIRLS
10 seconds	8 seconds

BENT ARM HANG CLUB

TEACHING SUGGESTIONS

1) Use the Bent Arm Hang Club as a motivator for a successful performance.

2) Share the club requirements with the students and emphasize that the Bent Arm Hang position must be held for the appropriate length of time. Select time for each grade level that meets the needs and ability levels of your students. See Bent Arm Hang on page 53 for teaching guidelines.

3) Take time within each class period to observe students who feel they are ready to attempt the Bent Arm Hang Club or use reciprocal teaching and have the students be responsible to observe each other's performances. Stress honesty and monitor performances on an informal basis. Commend the students for being honest and responsible, if appropriate.

4) Ask each student who passes the club requirements to print/write his/her full name on the appropriate grade level club sheet.

5) Give each student who makes the club a "special" Bent Arm Hang Club Certificate or sticker.

GRADE 4
30

GRADE 5
40

GRADE 6
50

BENT KNEE SIT-UP CLUB

TEACHING SUGGESTIONS

1) Use the Bent Knee Sit-Up Club as a motivator for a successful performance.

2) Share the club requirements with the students and emphasize that the proper Starting Position, Performance, and Finishing Position for each Bent Knee Sit-Up must be used. See Bent Knee Sit-Up on page 57 for teaching guidelines.

3) Take time within each class period to observe students who feel they are ready to attempt the Bent Knee Sit-Up Club or use reciprocal teaching and have the students be responsible to observe each other's performances. Stress honesty and monitor the performances on an informal basis. Commend the students for being honest and responsible, if appropriate.

4) Ask each student who passes the club requirements to print/write his/her full name on the appropriate grade level club sheet.

5) Give each student who makes the club a "special" Bent Knee Sit-Up Club Certificate or sticker.

GRADE 4

1/3	2/3	TOP

GRADE 5

1/3	2/3	TOP

GRADE 6

1/3	2/3	TOP

ROPE CLIMBING CLUB

TEACHING SUGGESTIONS

1) Use the Rope Climbing Club as a motivator for a successful performance.

2) Share the club requirements with the students. Make certain the students use proper and safe rope climbing techniques. Also, make certain you provide adequate padding at the base of the rope. Lastly, use some type of marking on the climbing rope to designate the 1/3rd and 2/3rd distances.

3) Take time within each class period to observe students who feel they are ready to attempt the Rope Climbing Club or use reciprocal teaching and have the students be responsible to observe each other's performances. Stress honesty and responsibility. Monitor the performances on a formal or informal basis. Commend the students for being honest and responsible, if appropriate.

4) Ask each student who passes the club requirements to print/write his/her full name on the appropriate grade level club sheet within the attained rope climbing level section. Continue to challenge each student to perform to the best of his/her ability.

5) Give each student who makes the club a "special" Rope Climbing Club Certificate. Include the three different climbing levels and place a check mark in front of the level(s) the student was able to reach.

BIBLIOGRAPHY

Anderson, Bob. 1980. STRETCHING. Bolinas, California: Shelter Publications, Inc.

Baltimore County Board of Education. 1982 A GUIDE FOR ELEMENTARY SCHOOL PHYSICAL EDUCATION. Towson, Maryland: Baltimore County Public Schools.

Bradshaw, Richelle; Main, Shirley; and Stewart, Gordon W. 1984. FIT ALL OVER: A Catalogue Of Exercises. Santa Barbara, California: 3 S Fitness Group Ltd.

Faulkner, Robert A. and Stewart, Gordon W. 1984. BEND AND STRETCH: Suppleness And Strength Exercises. Santa Barbara, California: 3 S Fitness Group Ltd.

Loken, Newton C. and Willoughby, Robert J. 1977. THE COMPLETE BOOK OF GYMNASTICS (3rd Ed.). Englewood Cliffs, New Jersey: Prentice Hall Inc.

O'Quinn, Garland, Jr. 1978. DEVELOPMENTAL GYMNASTICS. Austin, Texas: University of Texas Press.

Stillwell, Jim L. and Stockard, Jerry R. 1988. MORE FITNESS EXERCISES FOR CHILDREN. Durham, North Carolina: The Great Activities Publishing Company.

! FREE PUBLISHER'S CATALOG !

Send for a FREE catalog

of

INNOVATIVE CURRICULUM GUIDEBOOKS AND MATERIALS

in

Movement Education, Special Education and Perceptual-Motor Development

Write:

FRONT ROW EXPERIENCE
540 Discovery Bay Blvd.
Byron, California 94514-9454

Questions? Call 510-634-5710